Bjorn Borg
My Life

AS TOLD TO

Eugene L. Scott

SIMON AND SCHUSTER
NEW YORK

and Game

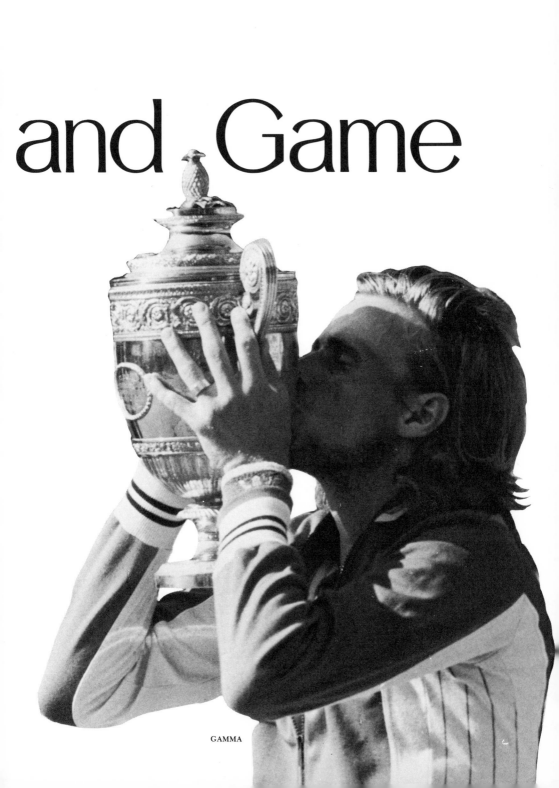

Published by Simon and Schuster
A Division of Gulf & Western Corporation
Simon & Schuster Building
Rockefeller Center
1230 Avenue of the Americas
New York, New York 10020
SIMON AND SCHUSTER and colophon
are trademarks of Simon & Schuster
Designed by Edith Fowler
Manufactured in the United States of America

1 2 3 4 5 6 7 8 9 10

Library of Congress Cataloging in Publication Data

Borg, Björn, date.
  My life and game.

  1. Borg, Björn, date. 2. Tennis players—Sweden—Biography. 3. Tennis. I. Scott, Eugene,
date. II. Title.
GV994.B65A35   796.342092'4 [B]   80-17322
ISBN 0-671-41207-8

For Lennart,
for my mother and my father,
and for Mariana

Contents

Warming Up

"You'd better do a lot with your approach when you play Borgie, because he's the world's best counterpuncher. Others may be flashier—McEnroe or Connors for instance—but Bjorn does more with the ball—more often—than anyone else in the game's history."

—VITAS GERULAITIS

To write the definitive work on the world's number-one tennis player when the subject is only twenty-four years old may seem premature. Many of Bjorn Borg's ideas and accomplishments are in the elusive process of maturing. For example, Bjorn's feelings about his mother and father and Mariana will add a dozen layers in his lifetime, and certainly the book on his tennis records at this point can only be an introduction to the eventual story. Still, Borg at twenty-four has already carved out a major niche among the greatest figures sport has ever produced, and the strong traits that have made him what he is are of great interest in revealing childhood and adult details that will one day be an orderly weave in the whole tapestry of his life.

More than several people were responsible for the chemistry that made this project possible. Bob Kain, of the International Management Group (Borg's corporate agent), was steadfast and enthusiastic; Peter Schwed, my tennis-wise editor at Simon and Schuster, who had complete faith in Borg and more faith in me than merely admiring my backhand lob volley; my British publishers, Sidgwick & Jackson, who went all out for us; Margaret Sullivan, who typed the manuscript and corrected more than one inconsistency, was encouraging and committed to the task with a tough deadline to meet; Mariana Simionescu, Borg's fiancée, who cooked many an extra chop or hamburger so that I could spend that extra hour with Bjorn; Lennart Bergelin, Borg's coach, who is so dedicated that he fretted I might interrupt his charge's training but soon learned I was as attentive to Borg's need for space as he; and finally to Bjorn, the most loyal and sensitive athlete I know, who remembered that I looked after him when he played his first men's tournament in the United States nine years ago and believed I would still look after him.

What is a "Bjorn Borg"? Underneath the iceberg, who is he? Does he bleed—inside or out? Most of what the world knows of Borg comes straight from the press. He has few intimate friends on the tennis circuit, though he is universally well liked. He is quiet and reserved, but no more so than 50 percent of the rest of the touring professionals. Borg's personality, however, is probed with a laser's intensity, because he is so completely his sport's number one.

Bjorn's shyness is magnified because his native tongue is Swedish, while English is the official language of every tennis press conference—even in Sweden. Borg's answers are short and to the point, and he does not philosophize or offer more than the answer to the question asked. This is true of most of us who try to speak a second language. How nimble do you think an American or British TV commentator or journalist would be if you asked one of them the weather in Swedish?

Throughout this book the words and ideas are completely Borg's as he told them to me. I have occasionally interjected a few words when they seemed appropriate, simply because there are times when a comment about a particular situation in which he himself was involved might be injudicious or immodest. Except for that, this is wholly Bjorn's book.

By far the heaviest volume of tennis writing originates in America, England and Australia, whose people are spoiled by not having to learn another language. At fifteen, Bjorn left school but still picked up a creditable facility in English. If he seemed clipped and cold in his early comments to the press, it was partly because of language and partly because he became the youngest male champion in the sport's history and yet has always been expected to respond with the clarity and depth of older tennis heroes.

Make no mistake, Borg has brains. Measure this man by his performance, perseverance or patience, or by his loyalty, or by his courage in crisis and not by glibness. The press has trouble getting Borg's short answers straight. For instance, it is still reported that his pulse rate is 35. Nonsense. The myth dates back to when, at age eighteen, he took a medical exam for military service and his pulse was recorded as 38. It is now about 50 when he wakes up and around 60 in the afternoon. It gets higher at the peak of a match, of course. That may surprise reporters who assume Borg is ice-calm because brine—not blood—flows in his veins.

EUGENE L. SCOTT

1

Me

Tom Wolfe's best seller *The Right Stuff* penetrates the extraordinary fraternity of space-age test pilots, whose guts and grace mean nothing without each other. Wolfe particularly eulogizes Chuck Yeager, the world's first man to break the sound barrier in 1947. Wolfe describes Yeager's moment of triumph—"He was going faster than any man in history. It was almost silent up there. He was a master of the sky. His was a King's solitude unique and inviolate, above the dome of the world."

That could have described Borg's elation after his fourth Wimbledon triumph—the identical isolation and glory. But victory is not enough to attain the elusive Olympus for either a Wimbledon champion or a fire-hot pilot. The quality of the man counts for as much as his heroic deed. Borg is made of the Right Stuff.

THE BEGINNING

I was born on Sweden's Flag Day, June 6, 1956, in Sodertalje (pronounced *so-der-tal-yeh*), a small manufacturing town of 100,000 people a thirty-minute drive southwest from Stockholm. You might say I started celebrating early.

I am Margarethe and Rune Borg's only child, and like

that of many Swedish youngsters my first love was ice hockey. At nine, I was the starting center for Sodertalje's junior team and had visions of playing for the national team when I grew up.

My father was one of the country's leading table-tennis players and in the summer of 1965 captured the city championships, winning a tennis racquet as first prize. He gave it to me. My first tennis racquet at the age of nine. The next morning I walked four blocks to the Sodertalje Tennis Club and was turned down for the beginner's class because it was too crowded. During the next six weeks, I did what every aspiring tennis player does to learn the game. I attacked with passion our garage wall, using it as a backboard. Every day I played imaginary matches between the United States and Sweden; if I didn't miss the ball for ten hits, Sweden won the point. Then a vacancy opened up in the junior program. For the rest of the summer I arrived at the tennis court at seven o'clock in the morning and wouldn't leave until my parents collected me at dark.

The role of my parents was perfect. They were helpful, but never put their nose into my tennis. I was obviously crazy about tennis from the beginning, and they gave assistance all the time but never told me what to do, when to practice, when to play tournaments. If they had gotten too involved, I would quickly have been sick of training, everything.

It's fine for parents to give guidance when you're younger, but once I was eighteen I myself knew what I had to do to be good. It's like taking piano lessons when you're very young. If they had told me I had to practice four hours a day and pushed it down my throat, I would have quit tennis.

The next summer, when I was ten, I met Percy Rosberg, the best coach in Sweden, who came to Sodertalje to scout two thirteen-year-olds, Peter Abrink and Leif Johansson. I got a chance to hit with Percy for half an hour, and he didn't seem too happy about my forehand, which I already hit with a western flick, the result of my father's Ping-pong influence. But he saw that I could hit a lot of balls back and asked me to train with him at the Salk Club in Stockholm. Soon I started going to Salk seven days a week. Five of those were training with Percy and the other two were banging the ball about

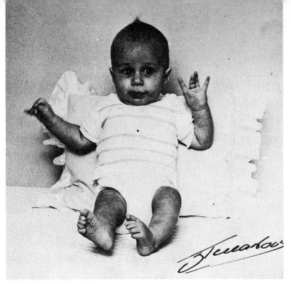

Above, my earliest portrait.

Right, my father, Rune, and mother, Margarethe, with me in the grocery store that we owned in Sweden before we all moved to Monte Carlo.

Below, the influence of my early passion for table tennis is still evident in my tennis strokes.

15

with anyone who'd hit with me. I traveled a train from Sodertalje to Stockholm for an hour and a half every day after school for five years. My parents would drive and pick me up at night, but I still wouldn't get home until 10 P.M.

For two years after I started tennis, I played all the shots with two hands. It was simply because my racquet was too heavy. At the Sodertalje Club, every member said that I had to change my strokes. Finally I did change to hit my forehand one-handed, but that wasn't enough. They wanted me to switch on the backhand too. "You'll never amount to anything with that two-handed shot," they all said. "If you want to be a big player you have to hit the backhand one-handed too."

The members got angry with me because I wouldn't listen. In the end I think that's the reason I've gotten so far.

It was important that I be satisfied with my game. I was hitting the ball well and beating some pretty good players when I was very young, and even though I'd tell the guys that some day I'd change, inside I knew I never would. Eventually I did convert my forehand because it seemed so much easier to hit top spin with one hand than with two.

From age ten to thirteen, I lifted weights twice a week —for hockey, not for tennis. But since that time I haven't lifted a weight. It probably does help some players with their arms and wrists, but I don't need the extra muscle.

Hockey helped me a lot with conditioning. It's good if you can play a lot of sports when you're young and then, when you get older, pick just one. Incidentally, it's fun.

I won my first tournament the next year at eleven, when I beat Lars Goran Nyman in the Sormland County championships. (Every tennis pro can remember his own first tournament win.) The next summer I won the championship of my age division in the Swedish National School matches. And the following summer, at thirteen, I traveled to Malen, in the south of Sweden, for the National Junior Championships, and I won in both the thirteen and fourteen age divisions. I was on my way.

When I was fourteen I was selected to represent Sweden in a junior tournament in Berlin, which gave me my first experience of international travel. I was hooked. With some

I'm the one kneeling, second from left, but I gave up my first love, ice hockey, when I was fourteen.

sadness, I dropped hockey to dedicate myself totally to tennis.

There was only one obstacle—school. The nickname given me by the girls in my class was Nalle ("Teddy bear"), but my teachers thought I was behaving more like a grizzly. In the second term of Blombacka school's ninth grade, I fell 'way behind in my work as I was concentrating more and more on my tennis. One lady geography teacher in particular had no patience with me and told me in front of the class that I was "lazy and stupid." I baited her and later refused to answer any questions, saying that she was right—I knew nothing. This possibly was my earliest training for press conferences.

The headmaster said it was not permissible for a fifteen-year-old to leave school, but finally after pressure from my parents and Leif Dahlgren, a top coach for the Swedish Tennis Association, the school relented and let me leave in March 1972 just in time for me to take off for the Madrid Grand Prix. There I scored the biggest win of my early life over Jan Erik Lundquist, a national tennis hero in the twilight of his career—in straight sets 6–3, 6–2. As a result I qualified for the Davis Cup team in May against New Zealand.

My first assignment was against New Zealand's number one, Onny Parun, who preferred to serve and volley on grass rather than to rally from the back court on the clay courts of Bastaad. But he was physically strong and I was a definite underdog. The match started according to form, and I dropped the first two sets, which took just over an hour, and was quickly down 3–1 in the third. At the 3–2 changeover, the captain Lennart Bergelin took my racquet and said, "God that's heavy" and gave me another one. I broke serve and won five straight games and the next two sets. I got unbelievably tired in the fifth set and was behind 3–0 before Lennart told me to play Parun's forehand more and to keep the points going. Parun was in good shape, but he didn't like to rally forever.

My tactics then were the same as they are now: keep the ball in play and don't make any errors. Slowly Parun began to lose concentration, and after two more hours his game had unraveled entirely. I came from behind to upset Parun 4–6, 3–6, 6–3, 6–4, 6–4 and became the youngest player ever to win a Davis Cup match. (Haroon Rahim was fourteen when he played for Pakistan in 1971, but he lost.) Two days later I won my second Cup match, defeating Jeff Simpson, 9–7, 6–4, 5–7, 6–1.

I loved the fact that the scene of my first Davis Cup glory was in Bastaad, a small seaside resort whose off-season population of 2,500 swells to 20,000 in the summer. Bastaad became the center of Swedish tennis through the generosity of King Gustav VI Adolf, who was an avid tournament player himself, and through the patronage of his father Gustav V, who played singles at the Bastaad Tennis Club into his eighties.

Congratulations from Gustav VI, King of Sweden, at the Bastaad Tennis Club in 1973.

My reputation for being cool under pressure started in the match with Parun. In the fifth set, I got a terrible call and didn't react. I told the press later that I wasn't bothered by referees or bad calls—that I just went after the next point. It was this response that caused the Swedish press to say for the first time that I had *is i magen* ("ice in the stomach"). But I wasn't always that way.

What was most important about my first Davis Cup experience was that it brought me into close contact with team coach and captain Lennart Bergelin. During the tryouts I was losing a challenge match to Ove Bengtson and questioned three of Lennart's calls. I even called him a cheater, at which point Bergelin went berserk, pushing me over the courtside benches and hurling a racquet at my head. I quit the match in tears and refused to practice for two days. The press criticized Lennart for "bullying his players and harsh discipline," but the complaints disappeared when he named me to the team.

Davis Cup training period wasn't the only time my temper got out of hand that year. I guess fifteen and sixteen are rough periods for many players. A month later I went crazy in the Championship Cup against Leif Johansson (my rival and neighbor from Sodertalje). In front of national television I questioned a call by stomping over to Leif's side of the court and circling the mark where my ball had hit. I lost the decision and the match. The press questioned whether Borg's true character was coming out. But that was the last real display of poor sportsmanship of my career. I regretted my conduct almost immediately, but was even more embarrassed that it had so upset my concentration that I lost the match.

If sixteen was an uneven age for my behavior, it also was erratic in the matter of performance. I had some good results, but nothing spectacular. I did beat Ove Bengtson in the finals of the Swedish Nationals to become our youngest champion, but most of my good efforts consisted of getting close—like losing to Roy Emerson in the U.S. Championships in four sets. The next season, 1973, was still unpredictable, but now my youthful promise had taken definite shape. In the French Championships, a few weeks before my seventeenth birthday, I upset the seventh seed, Cliff Richey, in the first round, 6–3, 6–2. His game fit mine perfectly. He couldn't outlast me from the base line and he wasn't forceful enough on his approach or volleys to prevent me from getting a solid whack at my passing shots. Next I edged Pierre Barthes, 6–3, 1–6, 8–6. The French hero was far flashier than I, but in the crunch he wasn't steady enough to play the percentages properly. Then I upset the U.S. Davis Cup star, Dick Stockton, 6–7, 7–5, 6–2, 7–6. Americans never do well in Paris; the last one to win was Tony Trabert, in 1955, and that's over twenty-five years ago. The French clay is slower than the American Har-Tru or Fast-Dri, which means that patience is at a premium—not a virtue of big servers and volleyers like Stockton.

The round of sixteen against Italian idol Adriano Panatta, was another matter. Here was a man who perfectly understood the subtleties of European clay. Not only did he have excellent touch and feel from the back court, but he was versatile enough to be a superb volleyer as well. Panatta won in four sets, 7–6, 2–6, 7–5, 7–6, and I played as well as I knew how. Panatta is an extraordinarily gifted athlete, and although he is one of the few pros ever to win the Italian and the French Opens the same year (1976), he hasn't the discipline to take advantage of his talents consistently. On pure ability—particularly the effortless style of his ground strokes —he is the one player who should be able to give Connors, McEnroe and myself nightmares, but he rarely does.

A few weeks later, I went to Wimbledon in what was the infamous year of the player boycott. Nikki Pilic, the Yugoslav star, was banned from Wimbledon by the ITF because he had refused to play Davis Cup for his country. The ATP (players' union) protested the ban, saying that players were free agents and should not be coerced into any competition. Battle lines were drawn between the ITF and all national associations on one side and the pros on the other. A court battle ensued, and the ITF won, but the ATP still decided to pull its members out of Wimbledon. It was a tribute to the depth of men's tennis that the championships went on as usual and broke attendance records despite the withdrawal of 79 ATP players. Only two ATP members ignored the boycott, Roger Taylor and Ilie Nastase. Britisher Taylor felt a conflict of loyalty between his union and his country's Wimbledon, and he chose his country, later suffering the wrath of his peers. Nastase, always controversial, told what the ATP considered more than a white lie—that the Romanian government had ordered him to play.

Only one Swedish player, Ove Bengtson, was a member of the ATP, and he was the only one who withdrew. I played and was seeded fifth, opening my first men's match (I had won junior Wimbledon the year before) against the Indian, Prem Lall, on the famous center court. I won, 6–3, 6–4, 9–8. (Wimbledon had its own tie break at 8 all until 1979, when they joined the rest of the tennis world by starting the breaker at 6 all).

I remember thinking how lucky I was. Hundreds of players came to Wimbledon year after year and never got a chance to compete on center court. In my first match I played and won on the most famous surface in the world. In the next two rounds I defeated German Karl Meiler and Hungarian Szabolcs Baranyi, both in five sets, to face Roger Taylor in the quarters.

The press went crazy over my success, although it hadn't been that great, considering the diluted field. The most famous headline during the fortnight appeared under Peter Wilson's byline in the *Daily Mirror*—A STAR IS BJORN. I lost to Taylor in five sets, 6–1, 6–8, 4–6, 6–3, 7–5. I had been down 1–5 in the fifth and fought back to 5–5, forty-thirty on my serve, when I was foot-faulted on a second serve, bringing the score to deuce. My concentration must have been jostled a bit, and Taylor must have felt that he had been given a huge Christmas present. He won the next two points and served out the match, after sportingly overruling a service linesman who had called a ball in his favor on match point.

Later that 1973 summer, I pulled off my best win over Ken Rosewall in the round of sixteen at the Canadian Open, 2–6, 6–1, 7–5. Rosewall, despite being thirty-eight years old, was ranked third in the world at the time, and I had come back from 3–5 in the last set. I lost in the quarters to Manolo Orantes, 7–5, 7–6, but played well and heard Orantes say afterward that it was one of his best matches of the year.

While I wasn't winning any tournaments, I was compiling a reasonable record of wins against higher-ranked players and felt that it was only a matter of time before I could string together more than one good win a week. And my most unexpected victory of the season came ten days later at the U.S. Open at Forest Hills—one of the last times it was played on grass. I upset Arthur Ashe, an expert on any slick surface, in the third round, 6–7, 6–4, 6–4, 6–4. It was the first time I had beaten a superstar on turf. I hadn't been expected to win; my serve was weak, and I had a nonexistent volley. But I could hit ground strokes all day, and my passing shots were deadly. The pitch at Forest Hills was the worst of any major tournament, which actually helped my game. There is nothing so helpful to a slow spinning serve as a patch of bad grass. In addition, the court was soft, which meant that my shallow volleys stayed low, preventing Ashe from taking a big swipe on his passing shots. The experience was critical in building my confidence that one day I would play well at the Mecca of grass tournaments, Wimbledon.

I always loved to play Ashe. Not that I always won—I didn't. The last match I lost at Wimbledon was to Ashe in 1975. He comes in on everything and anything—on a fast or slow surface—so the points are over real quick either way. He takes my second serve and chips it with his backhand to my backhand and lopes into net, where I either pass him or he volleys a winner. I love to return his serve. It's hard and fairly flat, which gives me a perfect ball to hit—unless it's an ace. Ashe is clever when he plays. He uses his head. They say I don't talk a lot. But what about him? I rarely get anything out of him.

STATISTICS

BJORN RUNE BORG

DATE OF BIRTH:	June 6, 1956
PLACE OF BIRTH:	Sodertalje, Sweden
RESIDENCE:	Monte Carlo, Monaco
HEIGHT:	5'11"
WEIGHT:	160 lbs.
EYES:	Blue
HAIR:	Blond
COMPLEXION:	Fair
NICK NAMES:	*Scumpul* ("darling" in Romanian), *Burken* ("can" in Swedish), *Nalle* ("Teddy Bear" in Swedish)
BEARD:	From time to time
MARITAL STATUS:	Married to Mariana Simionescu, Romanian professional tennis player, July 24, 1980, in Bucharest. (Note: The manuscript for this book was written at a time prior to the marriage, which accounts for the references to Mariana as Borg's fiancée.)

RACQUET BRAND:	Donnay, worldwide
GRIPS:	Forehand, western; serve, continental; volley, continental; backhand, two-handed Eastern.
RACQUET SIZE:	4⅝ heavy, 10-inch leather grip
GRIP TYPE:	Fairway, two leather grips per handle
SHOE BRAND:	Diadora
SHOE SIZE:	9½
SHIRT BRAND:	Fila
SHIRT SIZE:	Medium (40)
SHORT BRAND:	Fila
SHORT SIZE:	32
PERSONAL HABITS:	Always wears on right wrist gold bracelet with "Bjorn" engraved in a small square. Gold chain around neck (both birthday presents from Mariana) plus headband close to eyes. Sweatlets on both hands plus tape over knuckles and inside callus on left hand. Uses sawdust to dry hands; never gauze or glove. Wears thick wedding band on ring finger of left hand. Mariana wore duplicate as engagement ring, but narrow band was substituted on their wedding day.
CAREER EARNINGS *(1973–March 1980)*	$3,160,516*

* Does not include endorsements or exhibitions

For a long time I never concerned myself about the big money in tennis. The ITF prohibited any one under eighteen from accepting prize money, a rule that was only nullified when I was seventeen. The winter of 1974 I was tempted into signing an exclusive contract with World Championship Tennis (WCT), which organizes many of the major pro tournaments around the world. The Swedish Tennis Association was horrified that I would be forever out of Davis Cup competition, and so the President of the STA, Mats Hasselquist, devised a scheme whereby I would be hired by Scandinavian Airlines for five years and paid $100,000 a year and free travel around the world as a public-relations officer in return for playing the major Swedish tournaments plus Davis Cup. I also could play any WCT events that did not conflict with my commitments to the Swedish Association. Simultaneously the manager of Jimmy Connors, Bill Riordan, offered me a contract to play his USTA circuit, but I turned him down. I felt that, even without Connors, WCT offered the best over-all competition.

Nineteen seventy-four was the first year in which I was a factor at every tournament. Two weeks after losing the WCT finals to Newcombe in four sets in early May, I became the youngest player ever to win the Italian Championships. I played like a streak, winning my last three matches over Manuel Orantes, Guillermo Vilas, and Ilie Nastase. A week later, at age eighteen I became the youngest ever to win the French Open by beating Raul Ramirez, Harold Solomon, and then Orantes again in the finals after being down two sets to love.

I was wiped out physically and mentally by the time I reached Wimbledon and was destroyed by El Shafei, 6–2, 6–3, 6–1, in the third round. It was as if I wasn't there. I had one other poor result that year, losing to Vijay Amritraj in the second round of the U.S. Open in five sets. But I won Bastaad over Panatta, and the U.S. Pro in Boston over Jan Kodes and Tom Okker, and by the end of 1974 was ranked third in the world and had earned $215,569 on the court. Off court, giant offers for clothes, racquets, cars, beer, shoes and hotel endorsements tumbled in so fast that I needed an agent, so I signed with the American manager Mark McCormack, whose International Management Group clients included Arnold Palmer, John Newcombe, Rod Laver, Pelé, Jackie Stuart and Jean Claude Killy.

When I turned pro at the beginning of 1974, I interviewed Bill Riordan, Donald Dell, and IMG for the best agent to represent me. Riordan had his own circuit at the time and was a maverick tennis promoter, but I always liked his sense of humor. Dell represented many of the top Americans, but not any prominent foreigners. It was Laver who got me to sign with IMG. For me they're the best. When I play exhibitions around the world it is important not to play in countries that have giant taxes.

Bob Kain of IMG looks after me in America—he's the best of all the agents—and Peter Worth takes care of me in Europe. Vitas Gerulaitis once almost lured me away from IMG to set up our own company. It was pretty close. Then I decided that I had been with IMG for so long and they had been so good—why should I get into a hassle by changing? IMG's full range of services includes insurance policies covering injury, death, and disability for the rest of my life. They have even bought a ten million dollar key-man policy for themselves so that, in case I get hurt, they won't suffer from the loss of fees.

BJORN BORG'S EMPIRE OF ENDORSEMENTS

WORLDWIDE

Fila clothes (except
   Scandinavia)
Scandinavian Airline System
Diadora tennis shoes (except
   United States and Canada)
Tretorn clogs
Lois bluejeans
V.S. Gut
Saab automobiles

Power Swing teaching aid
Toy ball machine
Ektelon stringing machine
Bjorn Borg poster (two kinds)
Bjorn Borg calendar (two kinds)
Donnay racquets
Bjorn Borg jigsaw puzzle
Viking sewing machine
Suntan lotion (pending
   contract)

CANADA

Collegiate headbands
Tretorn tennis shoes

SCANDINAVIA

Bjorn Borg headbands
Jockey clothes

Bjorn Borg key ring
Bjorn Borg notebook, pencil
   and eraser

Headband

SAS Arm Patch

Racquet

Shirts & Shorts

Gutstrings

Penn Ball

Wristband

Socks

Shoes

FINLEY PHOTOGRAPHICS

This photograph shows certain equipment and wearing apparel that Bjorn Borg uses in actual play, receiving substantial sums for his endorsements. He also endorses a great many other products, as listed on the facing page. Borg's annual income from all this is in excess of $1,500,000.

EUROPE

Penn tennis balls
Pelican tennis toy
Kellogg cereal

Tom's chocolate bar
Bjorn Borg doll
Cosmetic line (pending
   contract)

SOUTH AMERICA

Penn tennis balls

UNITED STATES

Tretorn tennis shoes
Diadora running shoes
Caesars World properties

Bjorn Borg doll
Nutrament foods

BRAZIL

Bjorn Borg toy
Bjorn Borg soft drink

JAPAN

Sunkist soft drink
Department store boutique

My proudest moments in 1975 tournaments were victories at the French Open and the U.S. Pro—both for the second straight year—and the Davis Cup challenge round. But I vividly recall my defeat by Arthur Ashe in the quarter-finals at Wimbledon, 2–6, 6–4, 8–6, 6–1, the year he won the championship. Still, it wasn't a bad year. I ended the year ranked third in the world and $220,851 richer in prize money.

Over-all, that was a time of consolidation for me. I moved from Stockholm to Monaco with my mother and father to avoid the 90 percent tax bite Sweden was taking from my prize money. Rune and Margarethe helped me to open the Bjorn Borg Sports Boutique on the main street in Monte Carlo, where the weather was warm and the airport was conveniently close at hand when I had to fly to any of the distant tournaments on my schedule. I took absolute hell from people for leaving Sweden. I was called unpatriotic, selfish, and money-hungry by the Swedish press, which didn't ease my distrust of tennis writers. The only thing that tilted their slander to praise was Sweden's first-ever winning of the Davis Cup. I won twelve singles matches over the teams from Poland, Germany, Russia, Spain, Chile and Czechoslovakia, and lost none—which is still a Davis Cup record.

I love Davis Cup. The last Davis Cup match I lost was in 1973, when I was sixteen, to Orantes, 6–1, 6–2, 6–1. I enjoy being on the Swedish team despite the pressure of playing for one's country. But our team would be better if someone else were trained to play doubles. I'm not a great doubles player, but as things stand Bengtson and I are the best in Sweden.

One of my weirdest experiences in Davis Cup was in 1975, when we faced Poland in Warsaw. Because of the strict WCT rules, I had to be in Dallas for a press conference on Monday morning following the WCT finals. The only possible way for me to make connections, even with a private jet to London, was for my match with Wojtek Fibak to end at 3

Sweden captures 1975 Davis Cup. *Left to right*, Ove Bengtson, Birger Anderson, Capt. Lennart Bergelin and I.

P.M. on Sunday. If it wasn't over by then, everyone agreed, I would have to default. Sweden was leading in the tie, 2–1, and needed my point to assure its win. The pressure was crazy. I won the first two sets, 6–4, 6–1, when it started to rain. The Polish coach and captain wanted to stop the match, but Fibak was very fair to me and played on. I won the final set, 8–6, at two minutes before three. I didn't even change my tennis clothes. I put on my track suit and took a limousine to the Warsaw airport, where a waiting jet flew me to London. A TWA 707 was scheduled to leave at 5 P.M. We landed at Heathrow at five to five and taxied right next to the TWA jet. The TWA pilot knew what was up and had stalled for five minutes. I ran my bags up the stairs, the stewardess closed the door behind me, and we left. Obviously the rule was absurd, but I didn't have the confidence then to tell WCT owner Lamar Hunt that Davis Cup is more important than a press conference.

Birger Anderson was heroic for our team that year. He won one do-or-die match every tie. Against West Germany, the score was 2 all, and he beat Karl Meiler in straight sets in Berlin. He won the decisive point against the Russians in Yurmala. Then we played Spain in Barcelona and he beat José Higueras in the fifth match in five sets.

For three days before the Challenge Round against Czechoslovakia I couldn't sleep. Bengtson and I played the best doubles match of our career and beat Kodes and Zednick, 6–4, 6–4, 6–4, and I won two singles, and Sweden won the Davis Cup for the first and only time in history.

Afterward we went out to celebrate in Stockholm. You know, Lennart had long woolen underwear with tigers imprinted on them; he wore it for good luck at every match, regardless of the fact that it was 100 degrees in Spain and Russia. He wouldn't take them off. At the end of our party, Lennart jumped up to dance on a table and took of his trousers to display his tiger underwear.

In 1976 for the first time I started winning tournaments almost at will. I lost some important ones, notably the U.S., French and Swedish Opens, but I won more than my share, including the Canadian, WCT, German, U.S. Pro and, of course, Wimbledon, without losing a set.

It was also the first year that I got power into my serve. I shifted the position of my left foot, so my toss wouldn't shoot all over the place. Now I had to hit the ball out in front. I gained rhythm, consistency and power. I didn't watch anyone to get it right. I just practiced serving one or two hours a day in 1976 until I found out. I had never done that before. At the year's end, I had moved up to number two in the world and had won $424,420.

The next year my game was extraordinarily consistent. I had some major disappointments, again particularly in the U.S. Open, but my percentage of wins was 92.2. I won 71 matches and lost only 6, a world record. Wimbledon was certainly my most thrilling accomplishment, when I defended my title in a wild five-set final against Jimmy Connors, and for two weeks in August moved Connors out of the world's number-one ranking. My official prize-money count for the year was $337,020, which did not include $300,000 I made playing World Team Tennis for the Cleveland Nets for sixteen weeks. WTT had pursued me as early as 1974 to sign a contract, but Lennart thought the peculiar scoring system (one-set matches, 1, 2, 3, 4 points), the endless travel, and the over-all circuslike atmosphere would not be helpful at my stage of development. There was a general sentiment on the pro tour that WTT was positive security and valuable for older twilight players like Laver, Rosewall and Newcombe, but that the tournament grind was more competitive and better training. The single reason I signed in 1977 was that Mariana was on the women's team and we could live together and play tennis without interruption. Very few tournaments have mixed fields now, and Mariana and I would have been separated most of that summer had WTT not offered us both contracts.

Nineteen seventy-eight started out like a rainbow with my winning the Italian, French and Wimbledon championships in a row—only the second time ever that was done! But the U.S. Open once again proved to be my undoing, as I lost to Connors in the final. My ATP ranking slipped to three, but my prize money grew to $469,491. There are three or four sources for rankings in tennis, and it does seem odd that no single one is taken as official. The two largest tennis magazines—*World Tennis* and *Tennis*—separately compile records and come out with year-end standings that reflect the judgment of their selected tennis writers. The ATP every two weeks prints a ranking list that is based on statistics of the preceding twelve months. If you had a bad loss thirteen months before, you might shoot up thirty places in the rankings when that loss dropped off the computer. Players are now very clever about beating the computer system and often can calculate by sitting out a week how their ranking will improve drastically. Even the U.S. Tennis Association has a monthly computer ranking system, which is ignored by virtually everyone, except that it is used to fix the rankings of the U.S. players at the end of each year. It is ironic that for the past four years I have been ranked number one in the world by the year-end vote of the players, but only last year (1979) did the computer finally agree with that ranking.

Nineteen seventy-nine was the first time I started and finished the year ranked number one in the world on the ATP computer. My six best tournament weeks, without question, were the Pepsi Grand Slam, the French, Wimbledon, the Canadian, Tokyo Grand Prix, and the Masters. I won the Pepsi for the third time in a row, this time over Connors, 6–2, 6–3. Then I barely captured both the French Open and Wimbledon for the second straight year; no one has ever done this before—which proves how difficult it is to win on clay one week and grass so soon afterward. The finals of both could have gone the other way, with newcomer Victor Pecci having already beaten Connors and Vilas in the quarters and semis of the French. I finally nailed Victor in four sets, but only after he had shown it is possible to serve and volley on clay if you have unusual talent.

I remember they changed my locker space at Paris for the first time. Lennart, who is extraordinarily superstitious, went to the attendant and shouted, "What the hell is this? Why is it here and not there?" But I stayed in the new locker and nothing terrible happened.

My seventy-three-year-old grandfather too is pretty superstitious. During the 1979 French final, he and my dad took their fishing boat off Kattilo Island. They listened on the radio to my match against Pecci. If I won a point, my grand-

Opposite, Mariana and I celebrated my 1979 French Open triumph near the Eiffel Tower. ART SEITZ

father would nervously spit into the sea. Pretty soon he thought I'd only win points if he spat. I won in four sets, but he came back home with a terrible sore throat from constant spitting to windward.

I thought the Wimbledon final match against Roscoe Tanner would be very tough. You never know how he is playing until you get there. He takes so many chances. I've never been so nervous in a match before. Everyone said I was going to win for the fourth time, which put added pressure on me. When we started I was playing fairly well but not well enough, and he was serving unbelievably. Tanner barely missed beating me, but I edged home 7–5 in the fifth. Then I took an extended holiday in Monte Carlo and Sweden, mixing the beach with exhibitions all over Europe.

I returned in time to play the Canadian Open, which I won with surprising ease over John McEnroe in the finals. But it apparently didn't help my preparation for the U.S. Open. Despite five-hour workouts with Vitas for eight days before Flushing Meadows, Tanner got his revenge under the lights. I played well up to that point, and I'm not taking anything away from Tanner when I say his serve is improved 30 percent at night. You just can't pick it up early enough.

Assistant Referee Bob Howe had told Lennart two months earlier that I wouldn't have to play under lights. Then on the first day of the Open, Lennart requested that, if I had to play at night, to schedule me on one of the first few days, and not for the Tanner match; we knew that that would be the worst one, for sure. Lennart was then told we wouldn't have to play under the lights at all. Apparently, they didn't think ahead and reserve any good matches for the nighttime, and when Jimmy Connors said at the last minute that he wanted to play his quarters during the day, they put me at night. It's history now that Roscoe put my lights out in four sets. He banged over a dozen aces and another dozen that I could only return weakly enough to set up for his volley. My game on a fast surface is based on my return of serve. Take that away from me and I might lose to Tanner every time. I wasn't thinking about the Grand Slam. I wouldn't ever think about it unless I had won three legs and then had to change my regular plans to go to Australia at the end of the year, which is the time I normally rest.

> Borg is not given to making excuses for himself, but it is a matter of record that he has been unlucky at the U.S. Open. In 1975, when he lost to Connors in the final, he was taking massive doses of antibiotics for an intestinal infection. In 1977, he lost to Dick Stockton and had such a bad shoulder injury that he could barely lift his arm to serve. In 1978, he lost to Connors after doctors had advised him not to play because of a severe thumb injury for which he took two injections of morcaine, a powerful pain killer an hour before the final. And in 1979, he lost to Tanner's 140-mph serve under lights, which may be a worse handicap for him than any injury.

No need to think about Australia now. Just a few weeks of exhibitions and then the $300,000 Challenge Cup in Montreal and the Grand Prix Masters in January 1980, both of which I won. Those two totaled $290,000 for eleven days of tennis.

The Masters is promoted as the Super Bowl of Tennis, the last event of the year to decide the number-one player. (Except that it comes in the middle of January the following year.) The argument that football's finale is scheduled the next year is not relevant. Football's season starts in September and is over after four months, except for the Super Bowl. The tennis season lasts twelve months and then is stretched even further to accommodate a thirteenth for the Masters. It seems odd that we can't make a year of tennis last just a year.

Davis Cup does the same thing. First-round ties for 1980 were played before the 1979 Challenge Round was over. It seems ridiculous. Can't we organize a year's tournaments so they fit into twelve months?

After the 1980 Pepsi Grand Slam which I won over Vilas and Gerulaitis ($150,000 for two matches), and the WCT Invitational in Maryland ($100,000 for six matches), I won't come back to America for six months until the U.S. Open. It's not that I don't love the United States. Actually I like it so much that I may move to Florida before my serious playing days are over. The reason for not playing a full schedule there is that the tax burden is so heavy—50 percent for Federal and another 20 percent for New York State—that it's simply not worthwhile to play tournaments or exhibitions past those I just can't pass up for one reason or the other.

One of the things I like best about the United States is the variety of television shows. I don't understand Americans' complaint about the lack of their TV quality. They should see how bad and limited TV programs in Europe are. Do you know that people from Sweden come to the U.S. on vacation for two weeks, get a hotel room, turn on the color TV and never leave the room?

2

More Me

"Even if Borg weren't in the top ten, I'd admire him more than any other player. He never gives any trouble to the umps."—Anthony Levinson, nine years old, courtside aide at $300,000 Challenge Cup, Montreal, December 1979.

I don't talk about myself. Unless you count telling reporters what the turning point against Conners was, or telling writers that I played well or didn't play so well against McEnroe. I don't volunteer much to reporters. If they ask me a question, I answer it briefly, but most of their questions are impersonal or foolish, or both. They watch my matches, why do they ask me what happened?

A good journalist knows as much about the strategy after a five-setter against Gerulaitis as I do. That is, if he cares as much about his profession as I do about mine. In fact, if a sports writer charts the points, he'll know more about my strengths and weaknesses in that particular battle than I— until I myself see the stat sheets on double faults, aces, winning volleys, and so forth.

Most of the material written about me has come as a result of that crazy institution known as the postmatch press conference. In theory, the session makes sense. If every writer spent just twenty minutes with me after each match, I wouldn't have the time to play my next round. There are roughly sixty reporters in an early-day postmatch press meeting at the U.S. Open or Wimbledon—150 after the finals— which would take between twenty and fifty hours if I met them separately. The group meeting means that all questions can be covered in one short gathering—ideally a good practice. But the questions asked in those conferences are often moronic.

"How do you feel after winning your first Wimbledon?" (And the second, third and fourth?)

"When do you think you had it won?"

"How did you play today?"

"How old are you?"

"What tension is your racquet?"

These are some of the queries that draw short responses. My age and racquet tension are two that are particularly annoying, because both are a matter of public record and indicate the reporter hasn't done his homework.

My tag as a sphinx, I guess, comes from my not giving more than I'm asked for, and that's not much.

If I could speak in my own language, it would be much easier. To explain yourself in a different language is difficult. So, if someone asks me a question, I make a short answer.

The press conference is like a schoolboy biology lab in which a frog is dissected. The press picks apart Borg's anatomy like so many amateur probers, often with awkward motions and fumbling hands.

How can reporters have it both ways by climbing all over McEnroe, Connors and Nastase for boorish behavior and yet deride Borg for being emotionless and plastic? The Swede does all anyone could possibly ask of him on court. He is courteous, calm and serious about his work. He never questions calls or baits his opponent. Every official loves to work his matches, because he puts umpires and linesmen so utterly at ease.

Ironically, this sporting quality, instead of helping him, actually penalizes Borg by costing him as many as a half a dozen points a match. It is human nature to give a break to the complainer to keep him quiet. Any umpire who has ever worked a McEnroe or Nastase match desperately wants the event to proceed without incident. If McEnroe goes up in smoke on a close call at the base line and Borg is silent, there is a tendency to give McEnroe the benefit of the doubt just to keep peace.

The umpire, therefore, has the luxury of catering to the grumbler at the good guy's expense, which means that Borg loses on the tight decisions on both ends of the court. One example: In the first game of his final match with Connors at the 1976 Wimbledon, Jimmy served what everyone at court-side—except the linesman—thought was a fault. Borg said nothing. Ace for Connors. Next game, Borg served an ace past Connors that was close—could have been good or out. Linesman signaled good. Connors objected and the umpire called fault, overruling the linesman. Borg lost both decisions where he was surely entitled to one of the points and possibly both.

The press's only contact with Borg is at press interviews and on court where he is perfectly behaved, yet he is abused for not having personality—which is absurd. Bjorn has a wry humor, is mature, kind and warm. He is no Rhodes Scholar, but neither are Arthur Ashe and Cliff Drysdale, the tour's resident smart men. If one wants to talk seriously about Descartes or the world situation, don't pick a tennis professional. If you want to get your ears pinned back in tennis, Borg's your man, and the licking will be administered by the physical talents plus the intelligence of the world's most decent sportsman.

Tests of Borg's stature are everywhere. No one can ever remember hearing an ill word spoken of him by his peers. He brings out the best even among the circuit's dodgier characters. There are never any incidents in his matches, because players are too embarrassed to dishonor an athlete they know will give them every break.

Judith Elian, the revered tennis writer for L'Équipe, has known Borg since he came to Wimbledon as a fourteen-year-old junior and remembers that "even as a kid he had a sense of maturity. This probably was why he never became spoiled later by his glory and riches. Money and fame are distorting forces and you have to have an unusual balance in your temperament not to go crazy."

The question that I am asked most often is how I am so unemotional on court and why I never seem to get angry over bad calls. Well, I can go crazy over bad calls, but I keep it inside. How? When I was twelve years old, I was throwing my racquet all over the place and cheating all the time. I was a real nut case, hitting balls over the fence—everything. My parents were really ashamed and finally refused to come to a single match.

Suddenly I was suspended for six months by the Swedish Association. I lived in a very small town, and the news of my suspension spread quickly. People whispered behind my back about my being the "Bad Boy" of Swedish tennis. I took it very much to heart; it was a devastating experience that I remember as if it were yesterday.

Now if my opponent cheats, or if I get a terrible call, I don't say a thing. Inside I may say it all. But if I objected out loud, I know I would get so flustered and turn red that I'm determined never to do it. I guess the memories of my humiliation have stuck with me so that I'll never again do anything crazy or unsportsmanlike in front of a lot of people. I hope I wouldn't anywhere, crowd or not.

I think I get over my losses pretty quickly, which must be part of the same family of emotions. I also don't gloat over my victories. Once a match is over, it's over. I don't carry either the pain or the glory with me for very long. For instance, the day after I lost to Tanner at the 1979 U.S. Open, I had a two-hour breakfast meeting with my manager, Bob Kain at the Drake Hotel.

"Not many athletes would have adjusted to such a heart-sickening loss so quickly," Kain told me. "In fact, not many would still be in town."

There have been incredible changes in the game since I started on tour. The main one is that the quality of players is so much better. Five years ago, I played all the tournaments for two reasons. I wanted to make money and I wanted to please all the tournament directors. Now I just play the big tournaments, because the draws at even the small tournaments like Richmond and Birmingham are just as tough as the big tournaments. Remember those two Wimbledons when I almost lost to Victor Amaya and Mark Edmondson in an early round? The draws are now filled with players better than Amaya and Edmondson were then, and it's tough to fight through fields like that week after week. It's not so difficult for Amaya or Stan Smith or Brian Gottfried, because they don't win every week. I'm expected to. That's why I'm cutting down to fewer events next year to see if I perform even better by focusing on a few major tournaments.

For example, I have never prepared for the U.S. Open the way I prepare for Wimbledon. If I lose Wimbledon this year, I'm going to try like hell for the Open, because the "majors" are now my most important goals.

By pacing myself in this way I think I can play at least five more years. One day I'm sure I'll be tired of traveling, sick of hotels and planes, and I'll probably end up living in the States—most likely in Florida.

Once or twice a year I lose to a player ranked a hundred notches below me. When that happens, some people accuse me of tanking. One example was when, as the top seed, I lost to Bruce Manson in the first round of the 1979 Palm Springs Grand Prix. Let me explain what happened. On the Sunday night before, I had won the Pepsi Grand Slam at Boca West, Florida, 3,000 miles away from Palm Springs. I left for California the next day, flew for six hours when the plane suddenly was directed back to Houston because of bad weather. Mariana and I spent the night in Houston and Tuesday morning started again for California. I arrived at Palm Springs in the afternoon and went on court forty-five minutes later. And lost. Manson did play well. I tried but I was so tired I really didn't care if I lost or not.

There is no other sport in the world where the season is twelve months long and involves travel across the globe and back a half dozen times a year. Team sports in America have a limited season and require travel only within the States; and in golf too the entire PGA tour is played exclusively in the States. A few top players may try their luck in the British Open, but that's about it. Some might ask why, if I was so exhausted, I didn't withdraw. In tennis there is no provision, barring an injury, for withdrawal without facing a stiff fine. Besides, the pressure from promoters is intense to get you there in the first place. Every tournament director would rather have me play and lose in the first round than drop out. That way they can save face when confronted by spectators or press with the alternative of a Borg "no show."

Another embarrassment was my loss to Raul Ramirez, 6–0, 6–1 in the 1978 Tehran Grand Prix. Ramirez is a talented player, so I might be upset by him anytime, but the love and one scores were an indication that I was wiped out physically from traveling and playing too much. I wanted to go home. It's not an excuse, rather an explanation, when I say that my type of game from the back court requires incredible concentration and patience. It is difficult to operate at this level of intensity all year long without a letdown now and then.

> Mariana Simionescu was born November 27, 1956, is five feet five inches tall, weighs 127 pounds, has blond hair and brown eyes. She is a moderate-to-heavy smoker. She was ranked two in Romania for four years. She won the French Juniors in '74 over Sue Barker and reached the last sixteen at Wimbledon in '77. "The best match I ever played was against Virginia Wade at Wimbledon. I lost, 9–7, 6–3, but was really upset because Bjorn didn't come down to watch me play. He stayed on top of the tearoom to look at my match so he wouldn't get swamped by two thousand autograph hunters."

How I met Mariana is one of those ironies that amuse only me. Do you remember the 1973 Wimbledon, where I made up the story for the press that Swedish junior Helena Anliot was my girlfriend, so the schoolgirl mob scene might slow down? Well it wasn't hard to fabricate Helena as my girlfriend because she was! We went together off and on for five years, and during the 1975 Bournemouth tournament, Helena introduced me to her roommate. Her roommate? Mariana. I wasn't overwhelmed, yet I did remember her as shy and warm. The next year after I had lost to Panatta in the quarters of the French, Rune, Lennart and I decided to go out and have a few beers to celebrate Lennart's birthday. We drove out of the hotel and after about five minutes decided we might be in such bad shape at the end of the night that we shouldn't drive home. We returned to the hotel and hopped in a taxi. But first I went into the lobby and on a whim called Mariana and asked if she'd like to join us on the

ART SEITZ

Life on the road. Mariana does not like me with a beard, but I think it's too much trouble to shave regularly. That explains why half the time the public sees me with a beard and the other half without it.

Below left, Mariana has been holding my good-luck mascot since 1977.

Below right, Mariana wears more than her heart on her sleeve.

E. L. SCOTT

One of our favorite pictures, beard or no beard.

bachelor's night out. Mariana hesitated, finally said yes, and we've been together ever since.

For sure, we've had our share of quarrels. Some of them are pretty funny. Like the time at the 1978 Pepsi Grand Slam in Boca Raton when Mariana, Lennart and I were sharing a suite. Mariana and I had a fight and she said she was going back to Romania. I said fine. She packed her bags and left. Two hours later, Lennart and I realized Mariana wasn't there to cook dinner. We panicked. Lennart volunteered to cook some hamburgers, and in a few minutes the kitchen was filled with smoke. Just then the phone rang. Lennart an-

My "family"—Mother, Father and Mariana.

The score stands love–love.

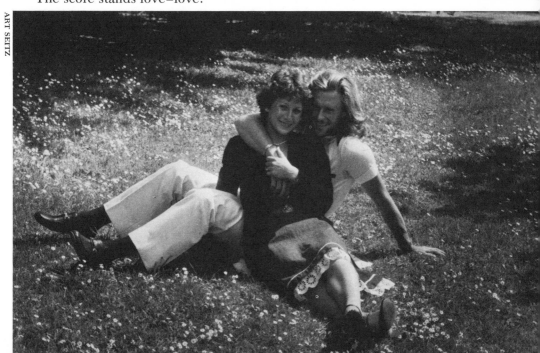

swered, talked for a while and hung up. Ten minutes later Mariana appeared as if nothing had happened. We all laughed like crazy, and Mariana went into the kitchen and cooked us a great dinner. She had taken a taxi to a hotel next to the airport and checked in before calling Lennart to see how the two men in her life were getting along.

In the beginning I believed you couldn't have a girl-friend and play good tennis. Obviously I've changed my mind. I love Mariana very much, yet I have no idea what it's like to have just one woman for one's whole life. I think it must be very difficult. If you see each other every single day, I don't think it's good. Sometimes I go to play tournaments without Mariana—the breaks make me look forward to seeing her. Sure, she is sometimes jealous. She knows there are women after me at each city for different reasons.

For the last three years we've traveled together just about all the time, which has meant that Mariana couldn't play the circuit. For us it makes no difference if we are married or not. We live together like a married couple now.

Every time Mariana and I come to the States, Mariana orders an extra bed for herself so I can get some sleep before the U.S. Open. The record shows it obviously hasn't worked. She's gotten superstitious. At the 1980 Masters, she decided not to order the extra bed and instead slept on the sofa at the Drake Hotel. The sofa was so uncomfortable that she didn't sleep for a week but I won. I wonder what she'll do the next time I play in New York.

It helps that Mariana was a good player, because she accepts the sacrifices. Another girl, who doesn't know tennis, might always want to go out dancing and to dinner. I can't do that and play my best tennis. Still I know it is a sacrifice for Mariana not to be able to have nights out on the town.

If I win, Mariana wins. Mariana appreciates what it takes to win and the preparation involved. Another woman might sympathize, but Mariana's level of understanding is higher. She never puts her nose into my tennis. I know what to do or not to do with my game. It's good that she doesn't involve herself in how I'm playing.

Sure we joke around. Before one Wimbledon final, I asked, "Scumpo, how should I play today?" "Serve and come in," Mariana advised. (Mariana's name for me is Scumpule and mine for her is Scumpo which means "darling" in Romanian.)

"I rarely talk tennis," Mariana explains. "When we are alone it's the only time we are away from the courts. If we start talking about tennis it's too much. What sort of relaxation would it be?

"The reason Bjorn and I waited to get married was that we just didn't know each other in the beginning and were so young. A lot of youngsters know their girlfriends or boyfriends from high school or college. We decided to wait and find out about each other. We've been living together for four years and so getting married will be no different except that I'll be Mrs. Borg and I'll call him my husband. And he'll introduce me as his wife. Some people don't seem to think it's a big deal to be married, but I think young people like the idea if they've found the right person. We certainly won't have children right away. It's too tough to travel with the kids when Bjorn is on tour. Besides Bjorn's not ready to be a father yet.

In Hawaii after the 1974 U.S. Open, I wasn't always playing tennis.

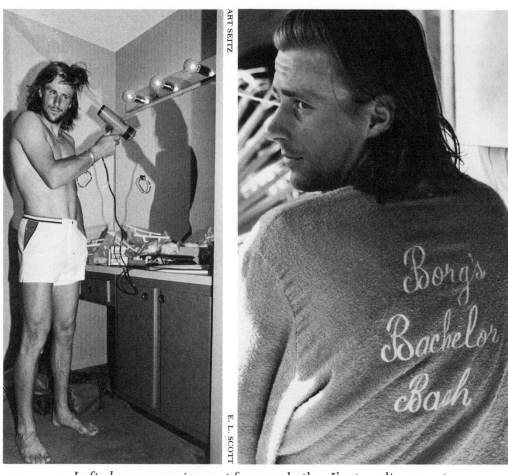

Left above, a requirement for me whether I'm traveling or not.

Right above, our wedding date will be recorded as July 24, 1980. Already on record, however, is the bachelor party thrown by Vitas Gerulaitis at his condominium in Miami.

   "All the guys on the circuit are his friends but the only one he is close to is Vitas. When single men are on tour they tend to make a lot of friends while the pro women can be very bitchy outside their proper cliques. When I travel with Bjorn, he comes home right after he practices or plays, so he doesn't have a chance to build many close relationships.
   "When he goes out on court, I don't know what he's thinking. No one knows. He may say that 'I'm just going to

play my game,' but I can't tell what's really going on in his mind. Off court I know, for sure. And I think I know why he's so great. He's an unbelievable athlete, and he's always in great condition. He sleeps so much, and he doesn't smoke or drink—except some wine and beer during our rest weeks."

Other than Mariana the closest person in my life is my coach Lennart Bergelin. I also have a close relationship with my parents—maybe too close. I've lived with them for many years, somewhat like Vitas Gerulaitis and his family. But now that Mariana and I are getting married, we'll make our Monaco apartment our home—at least for a while.

My nickname for Lennart is Laban (*Law-ber*), which

Lennart Bergelin.

means monkey or clown in Swedish. At first he got very angry when we used it—now he knows it's just being affectionate. There is a lot of teasing in our friendship. For example, Lennart never lets the phone ring in my room when we travel. He screens all calls by telling the operator to switch them to his room. In this way I am not harassed by friends looking for free tickets, reporters looking for a story, or teen-agers looking for some action. The phone rings so much in Lennart's life that he's gotten immune to the sound. Now when the phone rings on TV, Lennart gets up to answer it, but when it rings in the bedroom he's apt not to hear it. The guys in the Pro Shop a mile away could hear the phone it's so loud, but not Lennart.

Our most famous "telephone incident" happened in 1977 in Copenhagen, when Lennart and I sat in his hotel room waiting for room service. "I have to call my wife," Lennart said. He dialed the number and nothing happened. He then called the operator and asked how to dial Sweden directly. She told him to push the white button and dial the number. Lennart saw a white button on the wall and he pushed it. The light above us went out and he dialed the number. Nothing happened. Then he pushed the white button again and the light came on, and he dialed the number. Still nothing. He repeated the routine once more, the light going out again—before I pointed out to him that there was a white button on the phone too, and why not try that?

Lennart cares about Bjorn as if he were a bear cub.

He thinks that International Management Group pushes Bjorn too hard for exhibitions and he worries about an injury cutting short his career.

"The exhibitions are killers," Lennart laments. "At Frankfurt, the match against Vitas ended at three in the morning with ten thousand people still in the stands.

"It's easy to make the adjustment traveling from Europe to the States—two days and you're completely OK. The other way from Los Angeles to Monte Carlo can take a week of waking up at 1 A.M., then 4 A.M. and no more sleep. And rest periods to recover are nonexistent."

Borg disagrees. He has that flush of youth which makes him think he is immortal. Nothing can go wrong. If he has a week scheduled for exhibitions, he wants to play one every night despite the traveling that he must endure in the process. Here is an example of two weeks (February 25 to March 9, 1980) in the exhibition life of Bjorn Borg.

Mon.	Feb. 25	Caracas
Tues.	Feb. 26	San Paulo
Wed.	Feb. 27	Paraguay
Thurs.	Feb. 28	Travel
Fri.	Feb. 29	Chile
Sat.	March 1	Chile
Sun.	March 2	Buenos Aires
Mon.	March 3	Travel
Tues.	March 4	Copenhagen
Wed.	March 5	Copenhagen
Thurs.	March 6	Munich
Fri.	March 7	Munich
Sat.	March 8	Stuttgart
Sun.	March 9	Stuttgart

Followed by three weeks of rest.

It is estimated the two weeks will be worth a quarter of a million dollars tax free to Borg. The intricacies of arranging such a tour, including guarantees that the money will be paid—often in less than stable countries—is part of IMG's expertise. Borg has a dozen Swiss corporations, off-shore funds, and tax-free trusts to ensure that almost all taxes are avoided. That's true except in the U.S., which is the main reason Borg limits his playing schedule in America to tournaments only. There is no way for a foreigner to escape taxes on prize money earned in the United States.

Certainly it is more difficult to stay on top once you've gotten there. You must prove yourself over and over again. There is a hollow feeling when the challenge of reaching a goal is gone. The goal now is to stay there. It's like looking for excellence in isolation.

I know that most players play their best against me and, in a sense, this annoys me. My shots are straightforward and not deceptive—until a man rushes net—so a pro can plan and play his game.

Human nature is not happy with staying the same. There must be changes. Since the competitive challenge starts to fade with repetition, there must be a personal challenge from within me to keep winning major titles. The chemistry of a painter is different from a tennis player's. The artist is not judged as harshly as a tennis player. The artist does not win or lose every day in black-and-white terms as we do. Picasso did not have a 5–3 record against Van Gogh. On the other hand, I do have to live with my 5–3 record against McEnroe and try to see to it that the balance doesn't change.

CHAPTER

3

The Rivals

The casual spectator sees Borg as a blur of top-spin forehands and backhands, often not understanding the components of the Swede's genius. When Borg trades strokes with Guillermo Vilas, for any particular instant, Vilas is his equal. What separates Borg from his rivals is best captured in their own words. Each has striven to find an offense to penetrate Bjorn's immutable resolve, or a defense to frustrate his frozen concentration. Occasionally they are successful. More often they are not. But always they have a reaction to the experience of Borg's stringing them out in endless imaginary lanes crisscrossing the entire court.

Cliff Richey was the top-ranked American in 1970. He won the over-all Grand Prix in 1970, and that same year he was ranked number seven in the world. "In 1973 I was playing the French Open and was seeded pretty high. My sister Nancy [ranked number one in the U.S. in 1968 and 1969] was also expecting to do pretty well in Paris and asked me whom I played in the first round. 'Some guy named Borg,' I answered. 'Never heard of him. He's only sixteen.' I lost 3 and 2.

"I had also asked Nancy whom she played in the first round. 'Someone unpronounceable called Navratilova,'

Cliff Richey.

Nancy replied. 'Never heard of her.' Nancy lost 3 and 3."

Richey summed up his first and only meeting with Borg. "He had huge ground strokes. Compared to the other Europeans with good groundies—Darmon, Pietrangeli and Santana—Borg had no variety, no drop shots. Just *boom boom.* Even without variety he was good enough at seventeen to crunch most of the players.

"I don't know about comparisons," Richey concluded. "You know—who's better, Rod Laver or Bill Tilden or Borg? Laver and Pancho Gonzales at their peaks were too good to be rolled over by Borg. Pancho or Rod against Bjorn—all at their peaks? A helluva match no matter who wins."

JIMMY CONNORS ON BORG

I played Bjorn eight times last year and didn't win once. Toward the end we had some good matches—one in Frankfurt, one in Montreal, and finally the Masters. My game was picking up and responded to my feeling better mentally and physically. When Patti was pregnant I was worried, and when the baby was born, I wanted to spend a lot of time with him. My tennis suffered.

The adjustment was a big change for me. It took me time to separate my family and my tennis and to enjoy both.

To beat Bjorn I have to do what I do best—attack. But I have to be more patient and can't miss after three or four balls—like at the Garden (Masters 1980) we were hitting fifteen or twenty balls a rally, which is what the people wanted to see. The tennis was unbelievable, and I don't think there was a loser that night. He won the match but the experience is going to help me against Borg six or seven months from now. It made me feel that I can play against him again.

I'm going to come in because he hits so many short balls. If I hit my ground strokes deep and sharp, like I have been lately, he'll come up with a short ball more often than I. We both hit the ball hard, and it's going to come down to who misses an easy one here or there.

But I have to believe that I can hit fifteen balls in a row so that I *can* wait for the short one. I have to be in good shape to run down balls and to move the ball around. I've been working on myself physically the last few months—three hours a day in Florida against Eddie Dibbs, Harold Solomon and Fred Stolle, who pound me into the ground, though once we get to the indoor circuit with the restrictions on court time we're lucky to practice thirty minutes a day.

I have no idea how Bjorn wins Wimbledon on grass. He's not so comfortable on hard courts or indoors—the natural place for volleyers—and then he wins Wimbledon four times on grass, which is even a more natural surface for volleyers. I don't know whether it's a mystery to him too. Probably he's helped to some extent by the grass taking care of bad volleys —the short ones and the mishits are more effective than the good volley that gives your opponent another shot at the ball.

For pride reasons—he's beaten me in two finals—I'd rather play Borg at Wimbledon than McEnroe and the rest. McEnroe has a totally opposite game. He serves and volleys, which gives me a target. McEnroe can stay back and hit ground strokes, but they're not as penetrating. Borg is predictable. He's not coming in much. Borg and I are the same in one respect—that we hit big enough approach shots so that we don't have to hit a great volley. McEnroe will serve and volley constantly, which puts me in more of a rhythm, though he's difficult because his shots stay so low. Borg is tough because he hits so many balls back. He must have so much confidence winning Wimbledon four times. But believe me, they're both tough.

BORG ON CONNORS

We're not really friends. Not like Vitas and me. Connors is one of the game's quick men, and he works hard for every

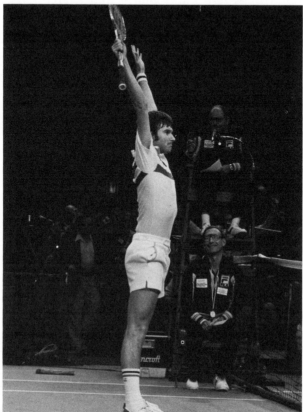

Jimmy Connors.

JACK MECCA

point, making him tough to beat. At first he intimidated me with his power, and he had a strong winning record over me, but I think I played him wrong by trying the strategy of other pros—to hit slices, soft and short to break up his rhythm. That wasn't my game. When I developed more confidence I felt I could hit the ball just as hard as Jimmy, and yet I was steadier. That was my game. And it worked. I played him eight times in 1979 and didn't lose once.

JOHN McENROE ON BORG

Left-handers will always give Bjorn some trouble. I think I have the perfect game to play him. Any two-handed backhand will be uncomfortable receiving my wide lefty serve. You have to mix up your pace with Borg. He likes the hard ball that Connors gives him.

He is always at the ball early. I'm not. He concentrates the whole match, and like at the Masters, if I let up for a few seconds and am late getting to the ball, he'll whip a few by me and the match is over. (Borg beat McEnroe at the 1980 Masters 7–6 in the third set.) You must be in good shape to play him, so you must prepare early the entire match and have the patience to mix it up with him.

I've seen him a lot of times where it doesn't look like he's concentrating—at Wimbledon, for instance. You'd swear he wasn't trying when he was down two sets to Edmondson and Amaya. Maybe he was nervous, and that's the way he combats it—with nonchalance when he's in danger.

I only met him three years ago when I got to the Wimbledon semis. But even in those two years he's developed a lot of personality. He's a lot more easygoing. With the people he knows, he's comfortable; he's got a good sense of humor. With others he doesn't think conversation is necessary.

I think he's going to be on the tour a lot longer than people think. Remember five years ago, when the experts said that with his type of whippy game, his arm would be burned out in two years? Four Wimbledon victories later, he doesn't look slowed down to me. He's got a strong body, and he can last indefinitely. It just depends on how much desire he's got. He's not gong to play that much this year, so he shouldn't get hurt. He's not "overtennising" himself the way others are. He can afford to pick and choose his tournaments now—unless something unfortunate happens in the way of an injury. You know, he's so successful at Wimbledon because the grass is not like a regular hard court. The surface looks after his volleys and makes them better than they are. He can hit a big first serve and stand on top of the net. He can drop volley or not even hit a solid volley and he'll win the point.

He stays back on his second serve and gets in a rally. He's the only guy I've seen who likes to get in a rally from the back court on grass. It helps that he plays most of his matches on center court, where the bounces are fairer and he can concentrate better. He's fast enough to be prepared early on grass too. He's faster afoot than I am, and although Vitas is just as quick, he often seems out of position. Borg covers court better than Vitas. You don't catch Bjorn out of position.

At the Masters, three times I gave Bjorn an off-pace short cross-court forehand. I figure 99 out of 100 times he'd miss it, but he made each one. I think I read him well, but you have to concentrate on every point or he'll pass you.

His serve? The first is damn good. He can hit that wide one in the deuce court and he can go flat. It's hard to pick it. I've played him when he's aced me once or twice a game. The second serve, he just gets in. But in the last two years he's developed more pace, so it's harder to attack. When I first played him a while ago, the second ball would go to the same place at the same speed. Not now.

Sure, we act differently on court. Once in New Orleans when I went berserk over a bad call, he gently waved his palms up and down to calm me down. When we play, the match is always going to be interesting, because of our contrasting styles, with me trying to rush the net and him staying in the back court. Sometimes when he and Connors play it's dull, because they both stay in the back court until someone misses.

The most satisfying place for me to beat Bjorn? That

would be the French Championships at Paris on clay over five sets.

BORG ON McENROE

His serve is the best. All left-handers give me trouble by serving wide to my two-handed backhand in the ad court, which takes me way out of court. McEnroe builds his game on his serve. If he serves well, his confidence grows. If he serves badly his confidence drops quickly. He is incredibly fast. Great power volley plus touch, with a flipping wrist. He can drop volley on both sides. It sounds strange, but he has more touch than Nastase. He is a master of the unexpected. I never can anticipate his shots. To beat him I have to keep him pinned to the base line by having perfect length on my ground strokes. If not, he'll come in on anything. I'd rather play him on clay, but I beat John badly on cement in the Canadian Open two weeks before he won the '79 U.S. Open.

He says he gets bored playing from the back court against me. I don't think he gets bored. I don't think he has the confidence to rally from the base line. If he stays back all the time, he's going to lose a lot of points. He has a great

John McEnroe.

serve and volley, but he can improve his ground strokes. We play a lot of exhibitions together, and I've gotten to know him well.

Despite what you read, he's a nice guy.

ILIE NASTASE ON BORG

Borg plays like a beggar. He doesn't give any points away. Never. Maybe he's the same way about his money. He's an unbelievable athlete. You remember when he competed in the Superstars Television event in Vichy he won six out of eight events including table tennis, soccer, canoeing, and the 600-meter steeplechase run, in which he beat the 110-meter steeplechase Olympic gold medalist. His legs are very strong. He's like Ashe emotionally—quiet, shy. If you left him alone in the locker room, he might not talk to anyone for an hour. But if you kid him, he's good and jokes back.

He can win when he's not playing so well—you know, hitting the ball off the wood, missing. Yet he keeps coming after you—so confident. Connors, on the other hand, can't win against the top guys when he's not playing well.

Ilie Nastase.

They should send Borg away to another planet. We play tennis. He plays something else.

BORG ON NASTASE

When I was eighteen and nineteen it was tough to play Nastase. I had no experience and got nervous waiting for him to talk nonsense to the crowd, umpires and even me. After I had played him so many times, I knew what to expect, and he didn't bother me. Sure, we are good friends. But when I go on court, I don't care if it's my parents. I'm going to beat them.

I have no hard feelings against Nastase when he behaves like a maniac. When we walk off court, everything is fine and we're friends again.

In the beginning he was difficult for me to play because I never knew what he was going to do. Maybe he didn't either. Every stroke was possible. His shots went anywhere, with all kinds of spin. Finally, my serve got better, so he couldn't attack and come in with that slice backhand approach that I hated. Also he used to let me come to net with short balls or drop shots, because he knew I didn't volley with confidence. I practiced the volley and the serve, and I pass off a slice backhand so much that Nastase can't hurt me anymore. McEnroe is more of a total player in that he can serve me out of my socks in the backhand corner and can attack with variety, but no one has Nastase's versatility of counterattack. He could hit winners from the craziest defensive positions.

VITAS GERULAITIS ON BORG

He happens to have a pretty good game against me. To hurt the guy, you have to serve really well, put away a lot of volleys, and play aggressively. More than a few times we've played it's been a close match, but he wins the big points. He does that against everybody! At Wimbledon in the famous match (1977 semis), I had a break in the fifth set and had a chance for another and also had a chance to hold my serve to keep the break alive, but he played good percentage shots each time—played steady and made me make the error. He usually gets a high percentage of first serves in; the second one you can still attack, but if you don't make a fairly good approach you're dead, because he has such incredible passing shots. I don't read him as well as some of the other guys do. McEnroe reads Borg like the front page.

I think Bjorn does have emotions, but he has a special talent for masking them. He doesn't let his opponent know what he's feeling. I've never seen him change his expression in all the matches I've watched him play.

I've been there on an outside court when he lets steam off; but his emotions run at a low level and usually the most excitement you get is a faint smile, but that's his way. I appreciate it even though I might go into hysterical laughter over the same thing.

You know he does have a great mental attitude, but his strokes are sound too despite people saying they're strange or unorthodox. When he's playing badly he'll just hit the ball a little higher and shorter, but it's always over the net. He always makes you play the ball.

I've never had a negative attitude even while losing to him seventeen times in a row. I always go out thinking I can get him this time, because I've played so many close matches with the guy. I don't think for me it's so much of a mental thing. It's just that he knows my game so well—better than what I've learned about his game.

I think he's got a good shot for a fifth Wimbledon title. The pressure is off after the fourth in a row. Everyone is puzzled how a clay-courter like Bjorn plays so well at Wimbledon. It's simple. First, he returns solidly; and the grass makes his volley better than it really is. A ball that he hits short or mishits—a flub volley—is a great volley on grass. He also plays the bounces beautifully. Everyone else is worried about bad hops, but they don't affect Bjorn. You need a lot of patience on grass, because sometimes you get so frustrated with the way the court is playing, yet nothing fazes him.

Also he prepares his strokes so early—quicker than Con-

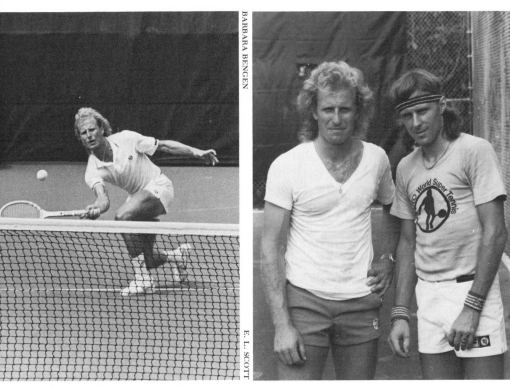

BARBARA BENGEN

E. L. SCOTT

Above left, Vitas Gerulaitis.

Above right, Vitas is my closest friend on the tour.

Below, even in the Bahamas, teen-agers flock to Gerulaitis and me.
Same thing at Wimbledon.

nors—which gives him another edge on grass. He stays back a little extra on grass and yet is fast enough to cover all the balls that come short. He is a great retriever. He constantly keeps the pressure on, because he returns everything. Most of us wait for cheap points on grass. Not Bjorn.

BORG ON GERULAITIS

In comparison with his play of a few years ago, Vitas' game has improved so much from the base line. I used to have a big advantage, because he had no confidence in his ground strokes. Before, he had to come in all the time, either immediately behind his serve or waiting just a stroke or two. He's getting tougher and tougher—he's so much more patient in the back court. I can feel, when we play matches now that he's a better player; even when I keep winning, I sense this. Everyone says that his big improvement is in his serve. Sure, his serve is better, but the reason he has finally beaten McEnroe and Connors is that his forehand and backhand are steadier.

The fact that we practice together all the time has helped him in two ways—one, that we hit hundreds of balls from the back court; and secondly, that he has gotten to know my game so well that it doesn't awe him. I won't keep beating him. Yes, I've won seventeen times in a row, but that's the luck of our styles. His fits mine perfectly. I love players to rush the net on everything, because it plays directly into my strength, my passing shots. Vitas is a steady and quick volleyer, not a "put-away" volleyer, so I always get a second chance to hit a passing shot. If we hadn't practiced all those times, the scores might have been worse.

If Vitas is playing badly, his forehand goes first. Then he backs up on this ball and hits it off balance. I think the reason I have beaten him so consistently is that he gets nervous against me. When we practice, he's not nervous at all, and he serves better—everything is better. We're about even in practice; sometimes he beats the hell out of me.

Vitas is much more serious about the game now. I know he stays out late going to Studio 54 and the Mudd Club, but he doesn't drink or smoke at all, so the next day he doesn't feel terrible and can still go out and practice for three hours after sleeping ten hours till three in the afternoon. And he doesn't fool around during an important tournament. He's my best friend on the tour—except, obviously, for Mariana and Lennart—and the one I spend most of my time with.

ROSCOE TANNER ON BORG

I'm not in awe of Bjorn. I respect him. I've beaten him and know I'll do it again. I have a plan whenever I play him and when it works, I win.

I must serve and volley well. I must take his second serve, rap it, come to net and hit a good first volley. If I float my approach or volley, I lose. He's accurate, fast, and has quick hands at the base line, not at the net. That's why you never see him at net.

He is the ultimate percentage player, so it doesn't do me any good to stay in the back court and rally with him. He's the world's best at that game. I have to take chances. I don't mind if I miss, but I must take risks if I'm going to break down his percentages. I have a chance by taking a chance.

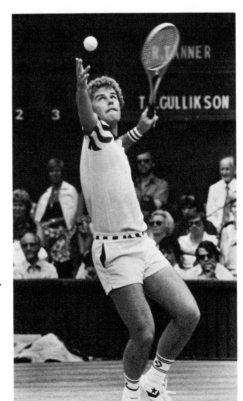

Roscoe Tanner.

Borg is the best not because of his picture strokes but because of his head. Connors has the purest shots.

I don't understand knock journalism. After Borg won four Wimbledons, no writer was satisfied. After he lost to me in the U.S. Open quarter-finals, the press asked crazy questions of Bjorn, asking him if he was going downhill, tarnishing his incredible Wimbledon record. I don't know how he took it.

BORG ON TANNER

I don't know him well. Maybe I should. He destroyed me at the '79 U.S. Open and almost knocked me off in the finals of the '79 Wimbledon. How I play against Roscoe really depends on how he is playing. He can beat anyone when his serve is humming. But he can lose to anyone too. He's just not consistent, which is scary to me, because I don't know what to expect. He takes incredible chances on his serve and ground strokes and if he's on, I lose; if he's missing, I'll win. Simple as that.

ION TIRIAC ON BORG

Basically, Borg is a more solid player than Vilas. You can beat Bjorn in only two ways, by attacking or outrunning him from the base line. Vilas doesn't attack that well yet, and Borg is slightly better from the back court, so how can Vilas win? What makes the situation worse is that Borg is so strong mentally. Normally, given Borg's slight stroking superiority, Vilas would win one out of three times, but because of his head, he loses eight out of eight.

It sounds like a contradiction, but what makes Borg so tough is his lack of diversity. He knows two things—backhands and forehands. He can't get confused wondering when he should serve or volley or attack. Also he moves better than Ken Rosewall. He's to the ball way in advance—meaning he's both quick afoot and anticipates well.

The final ingredient that puts Borg in the untouchable class is his percentage tennis. Vilas plays the percentages

Ion Tiriac.   Guillermo Vilas.

from the back court, but he's not as patient as Bjorn. Vilas is
not just playing against Borg now, you know; we're all playing against his legend.

GUILLERMO VILAS ON BORG

Borg can run longer and faster than I. A few years ago when
I was beating him, I was in better condition. But then he was
still growing up physically and was not at his peak.

He doesn't play many tournaments these days and seems
very fresh. He sleeps ten hours a day. When I lost to him so
easily in the '78 French Open I had a tough path to the finals
and he won his way easily. I was sluggish and was always
late to the ball.

MY LIFE AND GAME   67

It's better for me to play him on clay. His speed doesn't mean as much, because everyone has more time to run on slow courts. When I play Borg indoors, I'm always off balance. I can't attack him easily and he can run forever. The only way I know to beat him is to wait for the short ball and come to net.

He's very good at adjusting to strange conditions. He'll just put the ball in the middle of the court with plenty of spin until he gets used to the surface, wind, etc. John Newcombe once said that Borg's arm would wear out in five years because he swings at the ball so hard. Nonsense. Borg's body is his best stroke.

BORG ON VILAS

Guillermo is not as quick as McEnroe, Gerulaitis, Connors or me. But we play the same type of game except that I may do many things just a little bit better. Four or five years ago we used to practice together all the time. He was my best friend on the tour. Then Tiriac became Vilas' manager, and our relationship changed. He hasn't seemed as open as before. Tiri even tried to change Vilas' game by making him serve and volley more. Guillermo doesn't seem to have the same confidence as when he was staying in the back court. His great winning streak in 1977—ten tournaments in a row, including the U.S. Open—was all on clay.

His ranking has dropped to fifth in the world. Maybe he should return to playing as he used to, but I do think Vilas needs someone like Tiri to lean on. It helps him mentally.

When I play Vilas, it's strange, but I feel that I'm stronger, which sounds crazy, because Guillermo is such a bull. Yet I sense that, if we rally back and forth seventy-five times, I'm going to outlast him. Sure I lose a lot of points, but I have the confidence to stay with him forever. How can he hurt me? He can't serve and volley, and I can outrally him.

HAROLD SOLOMON ON BORG

Borg is the best athlete in tennis. His combination of speed, stamina, concentration and maturity on court is simply superior. I've played him fourteen times and never beaten him, in fact I have won only five sets.

Maybe there's something wrong with him. The last time I played him for over three hours and changed my shirt four times and looked at him and his shirt wasn't even wet. I've never seen him take a deep breath on court. I've tried everything. But each tactic I try, he does better—he's faster and has more endurance. One basic difference that might account for his ability to last longer is that he doesn't jump off the ground in making contact with the ball. His top spin bounces high, making me leap up in the air to return. I'm always reaching, and I am off balance 80 percent of the time. If I let the ball take its full spin, it's over my head. If I take it on the rise, I make mistakes. I can stay out all day with Bjorn and it doesn't alter the outcome.

The lefties and big servers give him problems, Amaya, Edmondson, Pfister, Tom Gullikson, Tanner and McEnroe,

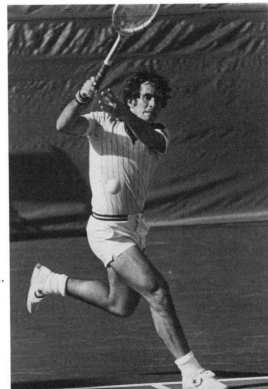

Harold Solomon.

but they had better strike when they get a chance, because he'll close the door pretty quick.

Borg is a true champion. He's our best representative. The best thing that's happened to him is McEnroe. That challenge will keep him going for big titles for another five years.

I remember playing him in Tokyo in '75. I won the first set six-love—just killing him. Tiriac came to the court and told Borg not to go for winners all the time. Borg won the next two sets 6–0, 6–1. He has animal instincts. His mind is clear enough for him to put everything else out of the way when he plays. He just lets it happen. Borg is an enlightened tennis player.

BILLY MARTIN ON BORG

Billy Martin of Palos Verdes, California, is only six months older than Bjorn, and when they were juniors they were heralded as the future of tennis. Both won Junior Wimbledon (Martin won it twice), both have blond hair, are not tall, and have beautiful ground strokes. The similarities continue down to their two-handed backhands and the fact that Billy

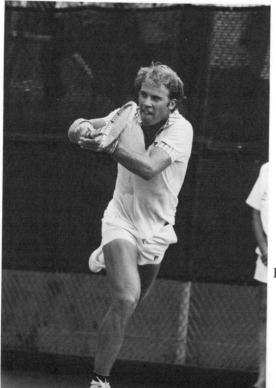

Billy Martin.

married a Swedish girl six months before Bjorn's wedding date with Mariana. As a UCLA freshman, Martin won the National Intercollegiates in 1975, and the experts predicted a dramatic rivalry between Billy and Bjorn and that they would share the International spotlight for a dozen years. It never happened. Martin ranks 60 in the world; Bjorn is number one.

"I remember playing Bjorn for the first time," Martin recalls, "in 1972, when I lost to him in the quarters of the Orange Bowl, 7–6, 5–7, 6–4. At 4 all, 30 all, in the final set, I came up to the net and my feet wouldn't move. He passed me easily. I didn't win any more points. I was physically dead and he wasn't even tired.

"The next time I played him was in 1977 in Cologne, and he thrashed me 6–0, 6–1, but I had game point in nine games. I played for him to miss at game point, which is a big mistake against the best percentage player in tennis. His confidence, his will, and his mental toughness are the most awesome in the game."

4

Coach

"I think Bergelin helps Borg from a confidence point of view and he takes away Bjorn's worries, but I don't know how much he helps with strategy—not that he doesn't know about strategy, but that's not his role."—VITAS GERULAITIS

There have been nearly as many lines written about famous tennis coaches as about their pupils—and not much has been complimentary. The most common words used to describe Ion Tiriac's relationship with Guillermo Vilas are "crutch" and "Svengali." Part of this is the press's natural inclination to be sensational and negative—else why wouldn't the first description of any coach be the more positive, like "aide" or "loyal friend."

The bad name given coaches is directly attributable to the media reaction to the personality of one man, Ion Tiriac. Before Tiriac, coaches were behind the scenes and faceless. But because Tiriac's behavior looked so sinister, first the players then officials ganged up on Tiriac. Did you know, for instance, that before the Tiriac-Vilas partnership, coaching on court during a match was legal?

In 1978, the International Tennis Federation adopted a no-coaching rule, but properly it should have been labeled the "No-Tiriac Rule." Without a chain-smoking, snake-haired Tiriac staring at Vilas with blank expression but with hand gestures weaving wickedly at crucial moments during Guillermo's matches, there would have been no rules change.

The new rule is ridiculous. Partly because it's unenforceable. Who's to say that Tiriac's sneeze doesn't mean "come to the net more" or that Dennis Ralston's tug on his right ear doesn't mean "play your man's forehand?"

"Of course the rules were put in against us," Tiriac says with a smile. "For that period in 1977 when we won eleven straight tournaments and fifty-eight straight matches, we were a helluva winning combination.

"Some parts of the game are more amateur than they ever were. Coaches can make the game go a lot smoother. The 90- and 30-second rules could be enforced better with coaches on court. If the coach interfered with play, the umpire could throw the coach out. Right now, referees are afraid of disciplining a player, because the star gate attraction might be dumped from the tournament. Coaching has improved every other game. Why should tennis be any different?"

Roscoe Tanner agrees. "The coaching rule is crazy," he insists. "This is pro tennis. Why shouldn't coaching be allowed as it is in every other professional sport. The classic and absurd argument for putting the rule on the books was that since not everyone can afford a coach, coaches shouldn't be allowed. Based on that rationale, because a guy ranked 250 in the world and can't afford to stay in a first-class hotel, I shouldn't be allowed to stay at the Hilton either."

It is ironic that of the top ten players in the world, only Borg (and his coach Bergelin) feel that on-court coaching should not be allowed. Ilie Nastase was himself once coached by Tiriac. Nastase now is just amused by the way the whole issue has gotten out of hand.

"Last week at the 1980 Volvo games in Palm Springs," Nastase says, "I saw Tiriac coaching Vilas on every point against Billy Scanlon. Vilas would try to hit a passing shot and Tiriac, talking in Italian, would say, 'No. Lob." No one seems to care about Tiriac's illegal coaching now, because Vilas isn't winning so much. I think it is a good idea to have a coach, in the sense that you have someone to look to during a match for moral support. He's a friend. Someone who always wants you to win.

"Tiriac has tried to change Vilas as a player—from a steady base-liner to someone more aggressive. Now you see Vilas underspin his backhand and charge the net. Tiriac has told Vilas about ten different service motions trying to make his left-hander more effective. It has confused Vilas. It's silly. Vilas has played one type of game for fifteen years, and Tiriac thinks that in six months you can switch everything around."

Coaching is a critical and colorful part of virtually every other game. Can you imagine football, basketball, boxing, soccer, or baseball without the wild ravings of the coaches? Knute Rockne, Billy Martin, Tom Landry are as integral to the history of their sport as the men they coached.

Coaches are divided into three categories; those who, like Nick Bolletieri and Dr. Alex Mayer, teach mechanics (grips, technique, etc.); those who teach the mental side of tennis (strategy, training, inspiration) such as Pancho Segura, Harry Hopman, Pancho Gonzalez and Fred Stolle; and lately another category has emerged where the coach performs part, if not all, of the manager's role. Tiriac is one example, Borg's coach Lennart Bergelin is another.

> Lennart Bergelin, fifty-five, is thirty-one years older than Borg. He is married and has three sons—Stephan, thirty-one, an engineer; Erik, twenty-eight, who may become a lawyer; and Nick, fourteen, still in school and not a tennis player of any distinction. Lennart was Swedish National Champion twice and star of his country's Davis Cup team for eight years. He won the German Championships on clay in 1951. Bergelin was coach and captain of the Swedish Davis Cup team from 1970 to 1975, but turned the job down in 1976 because the government took 70 percent of his coaching salary in taxes— and instead became Bjorn's full-time coach.

"I really started to coach Bjorn in 1972," Bergelin says, "when he first made the Davis Cup team. I never believed a player could stay home and become a champion. You have to leave home and play tournaments, so you can grow up to be a match player, not a practice player. You can see pretty quickly who is a tournament player and who is not. After a

With Lennart Bergelin after I won the $100,000 First Prize in the February 1980 WCT Invitational in Maryland.

year Bjorn was getting 75 percent of my coaching even though I was coach of the entire team. I never knew how good he was going to be, but the possibility was there early for him to be the best ever. We were together all the time anyway, so there wasn't much of a transition when I became his full-time coach in '76."

Lennart, although admittedly a simple and quiet person, is extremely outspoken on two particular issues. One is the matter of exhibitions, which he feels are wearing Bjorn down, and the other is that the U.S. Open is being played in part under lights.

"The U.S. Open is part of the Grand Slam, supposedly the most important tournaments in tennis," Lennart offers.

"They should be played under identical conditions except for court surface. Neither the French, the Australian nor Wimbledon have 'two gates,' one in the daytime, one at night. These events should be outdoor, daytime tennis. The nighttime schedule totally fouls up the athlete. There is no other sport where the athlete can finish at midnight and have to play the next afternoon at two o'clock. I understand the theory behind two gates—it's a way of selling more tickets. I just don't think that's as important as fairness and the player's health."

Bjorn agrees with Bergelin that Flushing Meadows is a nightmare at night, but he doesn't agree on the exhibitions. It may be difficult for Bjorn to be objective on the issue. He's young enough so he feels his body is immortal and wants to put away as much money as possible before retiring.

So, while Bergelin winces whenever he first sees Borg come off a seven-day run of nonstop exhibitions, he never lets his frustration interfere with putting his charge in top shape, including daily massage by himself personally.

Bergelin pinned Sweden's "Athlete of the Year" award on me for winning the French and Italian Opens in 1974. Lennart himself is the only other tennis player ever to receive the award.

"You know the Swedes are famous for their massage technique," Lennart says, "and although I haven't formally been to their schools, I have been taught by some of the best masseurs in Sweden. I have been working with Bjorn's body for so long that I know it better than the local masseur in each city who sees Bjorn for the first time. His legs are my primary concern now. He has problems from time to time with his hamstring and groin. It looks like at last he's over that terrible stomach pull during the 1976 Wimbledon. We know it came from learning the new serve, which required more power and more body turn. We were very frightened then—with those injections and everything—and very lucky to win."

Borg's relationship with Bergelin is more reliance than dependence. Bergelin combines the roles of father, brother and companion, without the tension that is likely to be in family closeness. Borg confirms his confidence and loyalty to Bergelin succinctly. "As long as I play tennis and want to win, I will have Lennart around.

"Although Lennart does not travel with me year round, he comes to every big tournament, meaning that his year ends after the U.S. Open in September and starts again with the Masters the following January. I can play without him, for sure, and did when I won $180,000, the largest singles purse in tennis history, at the 1979 Montreal WCT Challenge Cup. But this was not one of the tour's major titles. For these I need Lennart. He arranges absolutely everything so I can concentrate 100 percent on tennis. He fixes my travel, my meal time, my practice schedule, finds practice partners, even wakes me up—everything.

"In return, I pay all his travel expenses, meals and hotel bills plus a generous salary. In addition, he himself gives exhibitions, conducts clinics and endorses a clothing line. He also gets paid to work with the Swedish Davis Cup team. A lot of parents, officials and players have asked him to take on additional coaching assignments, but so far he has refused, saying that he thinks it's a full-time job looking after me.

"If you imagine that the job of managing a single tennis star is glamorous and simple, you're wrong. For instance, I hate to think of all the time Lennart spends on just one small part of my tennis existence—my tennis racquets. How many of you hackers consider that a club player is unbelievably cocky when he brings two racquets on a court? And if he carries three, he's a real hot dog?

"Last year in the French Championships, I broke the strings on sixty racquets in two weeks. Sixty! In the 1975 WCT event in Sao Paulo I went through twenty-eight racquets in six days. My racquets are strung at 80-pounds pressure, weigh 14½ ounces and have a 4⅝-inch grip. I play with Donnay worldwide, though until this year I played with the Bancroft frame in Japan, Canada and the United States.

"Silhouetted on my racquet strings was a large *B*, which most spectators thought stood for my name but really was an advertisement for the Bancroft racquet I then used. Silhouetting is a clever device by manufacturers to advertise their product far more prominently than the small label on the frame, which can't even be seen by the front row of fans. With my special stringing requirement, it is a nightmare to prepare enough racquets for each tournament. There is now only one stringer in the world I let near my racquets—Mats Laftman, who lives in Stockholm.

"It takes a unique understanding of the delicacy of racquet frames to find a pro who can even stretch 80 pounds of tension in a tennis racquet without breaking the string in the process or twisting the frame like a pretzel—let alone do it to my liking. Until recently we also had an American, Mark Williams, a pro at Jason Smith's Lincoln Plaza Racquet Club in New York, do some stringing. But once Mark was out of town, and Jason himself was nice enough to try. But Lennart "pinged" the racquets and could tell right away that a switch had been made. Lennart doesn't ever again want to worry about substitute stringers, so it's Mats exclusively now.

"As a result, the procedure for keeping me in enough racquets each tuned with the care and pitch of a violin is a giant headache. It means that everytime I travel to America and back to Europe I must stop in Copenhagen to leave off at least twenty racquets for delivery to Stockholm via SAS and pick up a fresh twenty for my next tournament. Complicating the matter further is that frequently Lennart is awakened in the middle of the night by a high-pitched, popping noise that means a string has snapped. Lennart has to get up and sort through the entire batch of racquets to remove the single set of broken strings so the racquet won't warp. The racquets can never be kept in the sun during the day nor near the air conditioner at night, or the pinging will be a symphony of strings snapping. When I haven't used a racquet for two weeks, I will cut out the gut before a match so a fresh stringing can be put in.

"Before 1976, Lennart used to scout players but now we never do. If I don't know how a player plays by now, I'll never know. I think it's a lot of baloney the way some coaches keep charts on opponents—that '64 percent of the time Newcombe hits his passing shots down the line.' So on a big point you cover down the line and he hits cross-court instead. Now you're mad at both yourself and your coach.

"When I was a lot younger Lennart gave me advice on strokes and strategy, but in the last five years he's more like a father. There's not so much advice now. I just want to see him around. I know how to play. We never have deep discussions about tennis, because he knows that I know what to do."

Some critics ask why Lennart hasn't coached Bjorn to volley, for despite his being number one in the world, he has done so without learning to be aggressive at net. If you watch Australians—Alexander, Dent, Masters, Marks, Edmondson, although none come close to Borg's over-all ability—every one is a superior volleyer.

"It's difficult to tamper with success," Lennart responds. "Tiriac is trying to make Vilas a volleyer and an all-court player. It hasn't worked. Vilas won more matches on fast surfaces by staying back than by trying to volley. It's a difficult question, changing the style of someone who has been comfortable in the back court for fifteen years. Suddenly you say he now must volley two points a game. You might destroy his effectiveness and rhythm. Coming to net when you're not used to it is like being at the frontier. You're fighting the unknown.

"The character of the player is important to determine his best style, his strategy. Tiriac is trying to make Vilas a volleyer when he isn't at home at net. Vilas won the Masters in 1974 on the Melbourne grass over Nastase and Newcombe, which was a great accomplishment. But what most people don't realize is that he did it from the base line. Connors and Borg have had great success on grass from the back court too. You must be very careful and patient if you're going to tinker with a man's style. You can't make gold out of clay.

"The toughest thing for a coach is to find what individual technique is best for this or that student. Everyone is different.

"Two years ago, two Swedes reached the U.S. Open Junior finals, but they won't sacrifice what's necessary. They have to travel, leave home and get tournament tough. Then you'd look at them; the ones who didn't adapt quickly, you send home. If they're unhappy with the life, don't force it. Some get homesick. You'll find out quickly. Bjorn left home and school early and loved it. He loved his parents yet wasn't always yearning to get home.

"Bjorn practices like he plays. He takes it very seriously. A lot of kids joke around in practice. Not Bjorn. He may just hit for an hour and a half with Gerulaitis before they begin to play sets. If they can learn to concentrate in practice where it doesn't count, think how strong their will is when a match comes.

"Tennis is a game of concentration. Was it good for Vilas for Tiriac to talk to him so much during the 1977 WCT Dallas Finals against Borg? Tiriac would say something after every point.

"Yet Borg himself didn't care. 'If you're a good player with experience you know what to do. If you're in trouble, you know how to change. One hundred percent of my game is instinct. I never stop and think I'm going to hit a ball cross-court or down the line. I just do it.' "

Bergelin has strong views about the harm of exhibitions on Borg's body. "Damn exhibitions," he muttered looking straight ahead, arms still folded tightly. "You can see it in his legs—tired." Lennart had just witnessed Bjorn lose the first set to John McEnroe in the semis of the 1980 Masters.

"Four times a year he takes off on an exhibition binge, where he'll play four matches in five nights all in different cities. Each night he finishes at midnight, and by the time he's had a meal and gone to sleep it's 2:30 A.M. The next day, he has to get up at 8 A.M. to go on to the next city. It's too much—the body doesn't recover from that sort of strain easily. Bjorn's a base-line player, so the exhibitions are tougher on him physically than the net rushers. After he's done an exhibition tour, I notice the effects a month later. His legs are slow and listless and he still looks tired and drawn.

"Sure, I know the money is tempting (Borg makes over $200,000 during a week of exhibitions) but maybe long range he could make even more if he planned his schedule more sensibly. For example, allow one day of travel and one day of rest before and after every exhibition. I'm just afraid he'll burn his body up the way he's going now.

"I should go to his exhibitions too. Bjorn doesn't want to lose to McEnroe even in an exhibition, because there will be a carry-over effect against John in tournaments. He must try to be in his best shape even for exhibitions. They should be scheduled carefully. Not this one-after-another-no-rest-travel-all-day-and-play-all-night sort of thing. If someone beats you a few times even in practice, it's easy for him to lose respect for you."

Exhibitions have been a problem for more than just the coaches. The International Pro Council, which runs the men's tour, has tried to eliminate the big-money exhibitions for years without success. The Council's view is that these special events dilute the fields of all Grand Prix tournaments, which are the game's backbone. They see a proliferation of exhibitions as potentially destructive of the tournament concept under the theory that if a superstar can make a million dollars playing ten weeks of exhibitions, he'll only play Wimbledon and the U.S. Open, and skip the rest of the circuit. The Council has been successful in limiting the number of exhibition weeks to six during the periods when $175,000 or more in prize money is offered, but fear that more restrictions would run afoul of American antitrust laws.

There are many theories on how much tennis a professional athlete can manage in a year without affecting his performance; if you play too much you get stale and risk injury, too little and you're not match-tough and also risk injury from not being in shape. What constitutes too much or too little competition is the core of debate, although there is general agreement that there are too many tournaments and that the pros tend to play too much. The reason is simple. Even when a pro is tired after six weeks in a row of tournaments, if a promoter offers an extra-large pay day for either a tournament or an exhibition the next week, the temptation is tough to resist.

The ATP (players' union) is always trying to establish new events around the world in order to create more "jobs" for its membership, which adds to the lure of staying on the tour "just one more week."

Complicating the question is the fact that no two players' schedules should be the same—some need work to be effective; some get stale if they play two weeks in a row. Adding more confusion to the equation is that most players and coaches plan their year at least six months in advance, slotting rest periods carefully into the tournament calendar. But they can't possibly predict how well they're going to perform half a year in advance. What happens if they have planned a month of tournaments and then two weeks of rest and run a bad patch of luck (poor draws, injury) or play badly and lose in an early round? Suddenly they're faced with two weeks of rest without having played more than a handful of matches. The solution is difficult, because the pros must sign up for events at least forty-two days in advance, which does not allow for slumps or the opposite—reaching the finals three weeks in a row and wanting a rest week earlier than planned. The rules don't allow for withdrawals at all, except in case of injury.

"In trying to find what the best schedule is for my own head and body," Borg announced at the 1980 Masters, "I am going to cut down playing in 1980 to ten tournaments and six weeks of exhibitions and see how my record is. My goal this year is the same as my career goal—to win as many major titles (French, U.S. Open, Wimbledon) as I can before I retire. It may be that by playing so little I won't be competitively sharp enough to play well in the 'majors.' If that is the case, I'll simply adjust my schedule to play more events in 1981."

Already there is enormous variety in the number of tournaments the pros play. For example, in 1979, David Schneider, Kim Warwick, Tim Wilkison and Ray Moore played the most Grand Prix tournaments, 29 each. The ones who played the fewest were Borg with 16 and Connors with 15. But the bare statistics can be misleading. John McEnroe only played 21 tournaments, but he went very far in all of them. He won 7 singles events, 14 doubles and 6 Davis Cup matches for a total of almost 200 matches—not including exhibitions—in the year. Clearly, he played more tennis than Schneider, who lost in the early rounds of most cities he traveled to. Indeed McEnroe may have played more matches in 1979 than any player in history—certainly more than anyone in the barnstorming days of Don Budge, Jack Kramer, Bobby Riggs and Pancho Gonzalez. McEnroe thrives on working hard, possibly because he didn't play that much during his junior years, but even Mighty Mac is showing signs of cutting down his schedule significantly.

Billy Martin, who is Borg's frequent practice partner, visited Bjorn's Swedish Island, Kattilo, four hours south and east of Stockholm to train after last summer's post-Wimbledon layoff. Kattilo is a dream retreat for a sportsman who cherishes his privacy. Actually it's one large island with a main house and five small cottages, plus eleven other islands with no buildings—and none permitted by Swedish law. There is one plexipave court adjacent to the main house and that became Martin and Borg's rock pile for four hours a day for a week.

"There wasn't enough excitement on the island for me," Martin recalled, "but that's what made it such a perfect place to practice. Lennart made sure there were always enough balls, water and towels. We had no excuse to leave the court even for five minutes. The conditions were perfectly controlled for training.

"I couldn't live like he does. I need to be around people. He likes to be alone. One thing about his island, he can get mad there and no one sees him. When we practiced, he smashed two racquets and screamed as loud as I did. Then he'd break up laughing. He could let everything that was inside spill out and wasn't afraid of anyone judging him.

"Practicing with Borg makes me a better player. He's so grooved that we can practice for thirty minutes and he won't miss a ball—which makes me try even harder. He doesn't need to do drills, because his rallies are like two-on-ones.

"One reason he rarely misses is that he has a simple game. It's not based on complex patterns or strokes. He just plays, regardless of his opponent's style. But I tell you, he would not be the same player without Bergelin. The combination of Lennart as a former great player and a "father" is rare. It's not the same with Vilas and Tiriac. It kills Bergelin if Borg loses. You get the feeling Lennart is playing Borg's matches too. I'm sure Lennart cares even more about his relationship with Borg than he does for his own family. I don't mean that Bergelin doesn't love his wife and three kids, but Bjorn has become another son who needs Lennart six months of the year.

"Bergelin doesn't teach technique, but he did help Borg with his serve in 1976. One of Bergelin's most critical functions is that he makes Borg relax—he knows exactly when it's time to work and when it's time to laugh and forget about tennis or a bad loss. The hardest thing for most players is not to worry about the next match. Bergelin prepares everything so perfectly beforehand that Bjorn doesn't have a chance to worry."

Fred Stolle, the former Wimbledon and U.S. Doubles titleholder is now a top teaching pro in Miami Beach, Flor-

Fred Stolle, former U.S. Singles Champion and currently Vitas Gerulaitis' coach.

Ever since 1973 I've had to have a regular police escort to protect me from overadmiring teen-agers.

ida. He is also Vitas Gerulaitis' coach—not full time, but whenever a big tournament approaches he is summoned to set the proper tone for a championship tune-up. Like a drill sergeant, Stolle harnesses Vitas' well known off-court energy to a stern regimen of discipline. Vitas remains at home with his mother, father, and sister Ruta for ten days before any crucial event in New York City. The late-night boogie at Studio 54, Xenon and the Mudd Club is replaced by four hours of intensive training each day, with plenty of rest; Vitas can sleep from 10 P.M. to noon without stirring the bedcovers an inch. One of Stolle's important tasks is to neutralize Vitas' entourage of friends. Gerulaitis is like a firefly and attracts dozens of well-wishers wherever he travels, and if it were left to Vitas, he would be having lunch or dinner with everyone of them the day before the U. S. Open.

Stolle changed that three years ago when he came to Vitas' house in Kings Point and discovered two friends bunking in the Gerulaitis household right before Flushing Meadows and expecting to stay the entire two weeks. Stolle threw them out.

Fred protects Vitas much in the same way Lennart protects Bjorn. It is difficult for either Vitas or Bjorn to go out for dinner without being hounded for autographs. Their simple rule is no signing until the meal is finished.

Some might question the value of Stolle or any coach when Gerulaitis has lost to Borg seventeen straight times. But the other side of that harsh record is that Vitas had never beaten McEnroe and Connors in seven years, and suddenly within fifteen hours during the 1980 Masters in Madison Square Garden, he defeated both, with Stolle by his side.

Is a coach necessary? Stolle thinks so. "A coach can't help much on tactics while sitting on the sideline. Even if he were able to signal his man, it wouldn't be worth more than a couple of points a match. But those points might mean the difference between winning and losing. Since I can't help Vitas while he's on court, I do want to pick up enough about his game and his opponents to offer just a few hints that could help him in a match. My advice may not help against Borg. Our strategy has never varied against Bjorn over the years. Vitas must attack his second serve, move to net and knock off the volley. Obviously, we haven't been successful yet.

"But against other players, it's different. Ten years ago, only a half dozen guys at a tournament could beat you. Now the depth is so extraordinary that anyone in the top one hundred can pull an upset. The reason is that the pros are practicing so hard. It used to be that the only guys on the circuit who would practice five hours a day were Roy Emerson and Brian Gottfried. Now the whole tour practices all day to try to break into the top ten.

"With these eager beavers, I can help Vitas' game plan by scouting rivals' weaknesses and strengths beforehand. But the main quality necessary in a coach is not his tennis brain. There are dozens of experts who can spot the same things I can. The important element is respect. Vitas has got to respect me when I tell him he can't stay out all night anymore. After the tournament I know he's going to waste himself a bit. I can't be his watch dog all year long. But if he won't pay the price when I'm in town, I'll quit. He knows that.

"Ironically, we know how to beat Borgie. Attack. McEnroe handles him best—hits that lefty serve wide to the backhand and comes in on his forehand. We've tried every-thing. Staying back, coming in on shots down the middle. Nothing has worked, because Vitas' style fits right into Borg's strength. You know they practice all the time together, and some points they play are the best I've ever seen. When they start to practice with six balls, they're so steady and fast they won't get to use the third ball for 20 minutes. Often Vitas kills Bjorn in practice. I think the difference is that Vitas serves much better in practice, and Bjorn rarely serves flat out until a match. Mentally Borg is something else. To win Wimbledon for four years without coming to net is one hell of an effort!"

5

Wimbledon

Wimbledon is a special flavor for me. For many it is a gathering of flowered hats and flowered pots, of strawberries and cream and champagne, and a grizzly hot dog called an Oscar. Wimbledon is a celebration more than anything else. Spectators ignore contradictions such as parking that costs more than admission to the grounds. Ninety percent of the matches the first week are played on field courts where there is no reserved seating. First come, first served—on park benches mostly, except that there is a small cement stadium on courts two and three, and at the south diagonal of the grounds sits court 14 with more than one thousand seats rising seventy feet straight up along the east tram line. But the world has only heard of center court, which seats twelve thousand— with standing room for another three thousand. This is less than half the number of fans Wimbledon admits everyday. Thirty-four thousand per day is not unusual, and in 1979 a record 343,044 came to watch over the fortnight. Where do they all fit? Seven thousand fit in a mirror image of the center called court Number One. The three small field stands accommodate another five thousand, and everyone else just mills about. It is not an unusual sight to see four thousand people outside the center court waiting for nothing in particular to happen—just standing underneath the English sun, when it comes out.

I love the English. They are so serious about their tennis —and everything else too. Tradition is God here. All matches start "at 2 P.M. precisely," even if there is a rain delay. The British always act so totally surprised when it rains—as if a downpour were as rare as snow in the Caribbean. All players must wear predominantly white, and we may not practice on the grounds during the fortnight unless we are scheduled for center court or court Number One.

Class distinctions do exist for the players, despite Wimbledon's attempts to see to it that all competitors are treated equally. It is true that the pro ranked 128 will receive one tea and luncheon ticket per day, limousine service to and from his hotel in London fifteen miles away, and full practice facilities at the Queens Club ten miles away from Wimbledon —the same as the Number One seed, but it is also true that there is an A and a B locker room, with all the stars quartered in A. Furthermore, if you win the Mens or Ladies Singles, you are made a full member of the All England Club with precious rights to two center-court seats each day.

Wimbledon to insiders is simply called the Championships, as if no other tournament in the world exists. I feel the same way. And not because the facilities are that great— they're not. The locker room is small and overcrowded. The lockers themselves are wooden, 10 inches by 30 inches—too small for street clothes, which must be hung on bench hooks. There are too few showers and the stream from the small nozzle heads hit you with blasts of water that feel like sleet on your back. And it does rain a lot in London, making practice impossible. Still, there is nothing like the center court for a final. The committee makes you feel that nothing is so important, and their organization has framed a perfect place for a championship match.

In the beginning I was not sure I could ever play well on grass. After all, before 1976 my record was not very impressive. In 1973, the year in which all the ATP players boycotted Wimbledon, I lost to Roger Taylor in the quarter-finals and the next year I was killed by Ismail El Shafei in the third round, 6–2, 6–3, 6–1. In 1975 I lost to Arthur Ashe (the eventual champion) in the quarter-finals, 2–6, 6–4, 8–6, 6–1.

I had a good chance to go to the finals that year. If I hadn't had a leg injury I might have beaten Ashe, then, in the semis, Tony Roche, who was past his peak. Maybe I'd have lost to Connors in the final, but in any case I was building confidence on grass. I had won my first grass-court tournament in 1974 over Onny Parun in the New Zealand Open, and this convinced me that even without volleying I could win on grass.

My only early success at Wimbledon was in 1972, when I won the Juniors, hardly an earthshaking event except that I did manage to enrage Buster Mottram, who was leading in the final set, 5–2, before I ran off five straight games and the match, 7–5. But until twenty I was considered a good slow-court player without a volley, and totally unsuited for the lightning pitch at Wimbledon. Furthermore, the International calendar is so peculiar that it schedules the French Championships, the unofficial world clay-court title, to end just two weeks before Wimbledon begins. The adjustment from clay to grass is awfully difficult to make in just two weeks. If you don't believe it, take a look at the record. Only two players in the past twenty-three years have won the French and Wimbledon the same year—Rod Laver and I.

The last four years that I have won Wimbledon, my practice routine has been virtually identical everyday. After Paris I rest for three days—no tennis, just sleep and eat. The French tournament is so tiring, physically and mentally, that I don't want to see a tennis ball for a while. Lennart, Mariana and I stay in Hampstead, a suburb of London, in a large suite at the Holiday Inn with two bedrooms, a kitchenette and a living room. It is forty-five minutes from Wimbledon, but it is worth the drive to be totally isolated for the world's most important Championship. Two minutes away from the hotel is the Cumberland Lawn Tennis and Cricket Club where, when I'm ready, I practice every day for four hours—two hours in the morning, two hours in the afternoon, with my regular practice partners, Heinz Gunthardt, Billy Martin, and Vitas Gerulaitis.

The Cumberland Club wrote me in February 1980, requesting an increased fee of $900 each for me and Vitas for the two weeks of practice. We need the practice, but we also give a free exhibition for the members which, in another country, we'd charge $50,000 for. I asked Bob Kain to offer what we paid the year before.

The reason I don't stick around Wimbledon is that they make it so difficult to practice. Technically, you're allowed only a half hour of practice a day the week before Wimbledon begins. Virtually every player ignores the letter of the rule and shares "half hours" with as many players as he can find. But it's still a hassle running from court to court so you don't waste a precious minute of sign-up time. As a former champion, I am accorded special playing privileges two weeks before the event, but often the courts are closed for maintenance or rain, so it seems better to be off on our own.

Some of my personal rituals are trivial, but we observe them with a smile just the same. For example, SAAB, as part of my contract, gives me a car in every city I visit. At Wimbledon the car must have a radio. In 1979, it didn't, and Lennart was so superstitious that he turned the car in for one with a full-blast stereo. Another thing, Lennart always drives, and I sit in the front seat, Mariana in the back.

Most of the time Mariana cooks all our meals; occasionally we go out to a restaurant or a movie, but not often. For breakfast she serves bacon, eggs, cornflakes, coffee, orange juice; for lunch nothing heavy, because we practice afterward—cheese, cold ham or chicken, milk or an English squash; for dinner, steaks and fish, and sometimes Mariana prepares a special Romanian dish, chicken and peas with a spicy sauce. I make sure my weight stays around 160.

"He's crazy about his weight," Mariana adds. "If he puts on two pounds in Monte Carlo during a rest period, he'll put on his track suit and jog 100 laps around our garden. He's also very superstitious. His parents alternate years when they come to Wimbledon and Paris. This year they won't visit Wimbledon, but will watch at Paris. Next year, vice versa, until the streak is broken."

My training during this period never consists of running. Maybe I am not always in tune mentally, but after two weeks on clay in Paris, I am in shape physically. We get up at 9 A.M., and after breakfast we are on the practice court by ten, where I rally for forty-five minutes or so. No drills. No set routine of forehands, then backhands; just rally. Actually, the first week, we may hit even longer, just to get the feel of the ball on grass. I hate drills. They're boring. I haven't drilled for five years.

> Vitas Gerulaitis says that "Borg doesn't have to drill formally. His rallying *is* a drill, because often he doesn't miss a ball for stretches of ten minutes at a time."

After warming up, Vitas or Billy and I will play four or five sets in the morning and another four or five sets in the afternoon. The Club orders a gross of Slazenger balls in advance for our sessions. We give special attention to return of serve, which I think is the most important stroke at Wimbledon. Sure, you have to serve well too, but most of the contenders already have good serves. Believe me, the difference between winning and losing at the Championships is return of serve.

One of the nice things about the Cumberland Club is that they will let us play on a wet court. Wimbledon shuts down the grass for practice at the first drop so that the turf won't be damaged. When it really floods down, we practice indoors at the London Vanderbilt Club, which is owned by an eccentric Hungarian, Geza Gazdag, who pioneered indoor tennis in New York City with his first Vanderbilt facility.

The only variation from this ritual was in 1976, when I practiced serving for hours. Both Lennart and I felt that too many players were taking advantage of my second serve, and that my first was neither forceful nor accurate enough. The intensive work on the over-all service motion was the most productive training I've had in the past five years, because it worked. But it almost didn't.

People ask why I don't play doubles anymore. There is a very good reason. The last time I played doubles in an important tournament, other than Davis Cup, where I *have* to play, was at Wimbledon 1976. I played with Vilas, and during a late-afternoon match I tore a stomach muscle, which was already sore from too much serving, and was almost forced to default the singles. But Lennart found a doctor, who said with injections every day I might continue. When I beat Vilas, 6–3, 6–0, 6–2, in the quarters I knew the pain killers worked, but I didn't consider what long-term damage they might do. For six days, an hour before each match, I received three injections in my stomach; they numbed my hips, side, stomach, and even part of my legs for several hours. I not only survived, I didn't lose a set in the tournament, but when I went into training for Davis Cup after a three-week vacation, my stomach muscles were still in very bad shape. I couldn't lift my arm above my head to serve without pain, and withdrew from the team for an even longer rest period. The next serious tennis I played that year was two months later at the U.S. Open.

I do like doubles, but in a big tournament, if you're trying to do well in the singles, it just doesn't make sense to play the team event. The matches are always scheduled at the end of the day, after you've played a hard singles and when you're most vulnerable to injury. At Wimbledon, they often have to play on the center court until 9 P.M., when it's usually cold and dank. The problem is that you may be on again the next day at 2 P.M. for a crucial singles.

In 1978, the day before Gerulaitis had to play Connors in the semi-finals, he had to play two doubles matches, the round of sixteen and quarters, both of which went five sets. He didn't leave the club grounds until 9 P.M. and went out to Connors the next day in a fast sixty-five minutes, 9–7, 6–2, 6–1. Vitas was a wreck against Connors—not that he wasn't in shape; Vitas is always in shape—but that competitive edge had been dulled by staying out on doubles court for six hours the day before.

Of the top six, Vilas, Connors, Gerulaitis and I never play doubles. Tanner plays, but without much success. McEnroe is the best doubles player in the world, and he feels it helps his singles, but that's for two reasons. John doesn't like to practice, and the doubles gives him extra court time which the rest of us get in practice. Besides, he's young, energetic,

THE GENTLEMEN'S SINGLES CHAMPIONSHIP

Final result: 6-4, 6-2, 9-7.

First Round

No.	Player	Country
1	A. R. Ashe①	(U.S.A.)
2	F. Taygan	(S.A.)
3	J. M. Yuill	(S.A.)
4	A. J. Stone	(A.)
5	R. J. Moore	(S.A.)
6	M. R. Edmondson	(A.)
7	J. Royappa	(IN.)
8	M. J. Farrell	(G.B.)
9	J. Holecek	(Stateless)
10	V. Gerulaitis	(U.S.A.)
11	M. Cox	(G.B.)
12	A. Munoz	(SP.)
13	W. W. Martin	(U.S.A.)
14	S. E. Stewart	(U.S.A.)
15	C. Dowdeswell	(RH.)
16	S. Krulevitz	(U.S.A.)
17	R. Ramirez⑧	(M.)
18	C. P. Kachel	(A.)
19	N. J. Holmes	(U.S.A.)
20	M. D. Wayman	(G.B.)
21	K. Meiler	(G.)
22	K. Cahill	(U.S.A.)
23	C. O. Ruffels	(A.)
24	J. H. McManus	(U.S.A.)
25	J. D. Newcombe⑯	(A.)
26	J. S. Hagey	(U.S.A.)
27	J. W. Feaver	(G.B.)
28	H. J. Bunis	(U.S.A.)
29	B. Mitton	(S.A.)
30	E. Deblicker	(F.)
31	S. Menon	(IN.)
32	R. Taylor	(G.B.)
33	I. Nastase①	(RU.)
34	N. Spear	(YU.)
35	L. Alvarez	(SP.)
36	Z. Franulovic	(YU.)
37	B. E. Fairlie	(N.Z.)
38	G. Masters	(A.)
39	K. G. Warwick	(A.)
40	R. Cano	(ARG.)
41	J. Fillol⑩	(CH.)
42	R. Thung	(NTH.)
43	P. F. McNamee	(A.)
44	R. L. Case	(N.Z.)
45	C. J. Lewis	(CZ.)
46	J. Hrebec	(CZ.)
47	G. Alexander	(A.)
48	O. Parun	(N.Z.)
49	A. Panatta⑤	(IT.)
50	Andrew	(V.)
51	D. H. Collings	(A.)
52	R. A. J. Hewitt	(S.A.)
53	F. Jauffret	(F.)
54	V. Amritraj	(IN.)
55	V. Kamiwazumi	(J.)
56	C. M. Pasarell	(U.S.A.)
57	T. S. Okker⑦	(NTH.)
58	A. Mayer	(U.S.A.)
59	J. R. Ganzabal	(ARG.)
60	V. C. Amaya	(U.S.A.)
61	E. J. van Dillen	(U.S.A.)
62	A. J. Pattison	(RH.)
63	P. C. Dent	(A.)
64	J. M. Lloyd	(G.B.)

Second Round

- A. R. Ashe① 7-5 6-4 7-5
- A. J. Stone 6-4 4-6 6-1
- M. R. Edmondson 8-9 9-7 6-3
- M. J. Farrell 6-4 6-2 6-4
- V. Gerulaitis 7-5 6-1 7-5
- M. Cox 6-4 9-8 6-4
- W. W. Martin 7-9 6-2 8-6
- S. Krulevitz 3-6 6-3 8-6
- R. Ramirez⑧ 6-3 9-8
- M. D. Wayman 6-3 6-4 3-6 6-0
- K. Meiler 6-8 9-7 3-6 6-3
- R. O. Ruffels 9-7 6-1 6-1
- J. D. Newcombe⑯ 8-9
- J. W. Feaver 6-1 1-6 6-2 7-5
- B. Mitton 7-5 6-2 1-6 6-4
- S. Menon 5-7 6-2 9-8 2-6 10-8
- I. Nastase① 6-2 6-3 6-2
- Z. Franulovic 6-2 6-4 6-2
- G. Masters 6-4 6-2 6-0
- K. G. Warwick 6-4 6-2 6-1
- J. Fillol⑩ 6-1 6-2 6-3
- R. L. Case 6-3 9-8 6-2
- C. J. Lewis 8-6 3-6 7-5 rtd.
- O. Parun 2-6 9-8 9-7 1-6 6-2
- A. Panatta⑤ 4-6 6-4 7-5
- D. H. Collings 4-6 7-5 2-0 rtd.
- V. Amritraj 9-8 6-3 6-4
- C. M. Pasarell 6-3 6-1 6-3
- T. S. Okker⑦ 6-3 6-2 6-4
- V. C. Amaya 6-3 6-4 6-4
- A. J. Pattison 6-3 3-6 7-5 6-3 9-8
- P. C. Dent 4-6 5-7 6-3 9-8 7-5

Third Round

- A. R. Ashe① 7-5 8-9 9-7 7-5
- M. R. Edmondson 9-8 9-7 6-4
- V. Gerulaitis 6-3 6-4 6-4
- S. Krulevitz 6-2 6-3 4-6 9-8
- R. Ramirez⑧ 6-4 8-9 6-4 6-3
- K. Meiler 6-8 6-2 8-6
- J. D. Newcombe⑯ 6-3 3-6 8-9 6-4 6-4
- B. Mitton 8-6 6-2 6-1
- I. Nastase① 6-1 7-5 6-3
- K. G. Warwick 7-5 6-4 6-4
- J. Fillol⑩ 8-9 6-4 6-8 9-8 6-2
- O. Parun 6-3 6-4 6-2
- A. Panatta⑤ 9-7 6-1
- C. M. Pasarell 6-2 6-4
- T. S. Okker⑦ 9-7 6-2 6-3
- P. C. Dent 6-2 7-5

Fourth Round

- A. R. Ashe① 7-5 6-2 8-6
- V. Gerulaitis 6-2 6-2 6-1
- R. Ramirez⑧ 6-2 7-5 6-1
- B. Mitton 3-6 9-8 9-8
- I. Nastase① 8-6 7-5 6-4
- O. Parun 7-5 6-4 6-4
- C. M. Pasarell 8-9 4-6 6-4 7-5 6-4
- P. C. Dent 6-4 9-8 6-4

Fifth Round

- V. Gerulaitis 4-6 8-9 6-4 6-3 6-4
- R. Ramirez⑧ 9-8 3-6 6-1 6-1
- I. Nastase① 7-5 6-4 6-3
- C. M. Pasarell 2-6 4-6 6-4 6-0 7-5

Semi-Final

- R. Ramirez⑧ 4-6 6-4 6-2 6-4
- I. Nastase① 6-4 6-2 6-3

Final

- I. Nastase① 6-2 9-7 6-3

Champion: B. Borg④ 6-4 9-8 6-4

Semifinals:
- B. Borg④ 6-3 6-0 6-2
- R. Tanner⑦ 6-4 6-2 8-6

Quarterfinals:
- G. Vilas④ 3-6 5-7 6-3 6-4
- B. Borg④ 6-2 7-5
- R. Tanner⑦ 6-3 6-4 6-4
- J. S. Connors② 6-4 6-1 6-3

Fourth round:
- A. D. Roche⑩ 6-4 3-6 6-2 6-1
- G. Vilas④ 7-5 6-2 6-4
- B. E. Gottfried⑨ 6-3 6-1 3-6 4-6 6-1
- B. Borg④ 6-4 6-4
- N. Pilic 3-6 6-4 6-3
- R. Tanner⑦ 8-9 6-3 6-2
- S. R. Smith⑧ 8-6 3-6 6-1 6-1
- J. S. Connors② 6-4 6-0 6-3

#	Player	Country	First round	Second round	Third round
65	W. Fibak	(POL.)	W. Fibak 8-6 6-1 3-6 6-1	U. Pinner 6-3 9-8 6-3	A. D. Roche⑩ 6-4 3-6 6-2 6-1
66	J. T. Whitlinger	(U.S.A.)			
67	H. Kary	(AU.)	U. Pinner 6-8 6-1 6-4 7-9 6-3		
68	U. Pinner	(G.)			
69	G. E. Reid	(U.S.A.)	G. E. Reid 6-4 5-7 6-3	A. D. Roche⑩ 6-4 6-2 6-4	
70	I. Molina	(COL.)			
71	S. Ball	(A.)	A. D. Roche⑩ 9-8 9-8		
72	A. D. Roche⑩	(A.)			
73	G. Mayer	(U.S.A.)	A. Metreveli 6-2 5-0 rtd.	A. Metreveli 6-8 6-3 6-4 3-6 11-9	G. Vilas④ 7-5 6-2 6-4
74	A. Metreveli	(U.S.S.R.)			
75	W. Lloyd	(A.)	R. L. Stockton 6-3 6-4 6-3		
76	R. L. Stockton	(U.S.A.)			
77	G. Goven	(F.)	H. Rahim 7-5 6-2 6-4	G. Vilas④ 9-7 6-3 6-4	
78	B. J. Phillips-Moore	(P.)			
79	H. Rahim	(P.)	G. Vilas④ 6-3 6-1 6-4...		
80	G. Vilas④	(ARG.)			
81	M. Estep	(U.S.A.)	T. W. Gorman 7-9 6-2 6-4	R. C. Lutz 6-1 8-9 6-3 2-6 6-4	B. E. Gottfried⑨ 6-3 6-1 3-6 4-6 6-1
82	T. W. Gorman	(U.S.A.)			
83	J. Borowiak	(U.S.A.)	R. C. Lutz 4-6 6-4 6-4		
84	R. C. Lutz	(U.S.A.)			
85	R. J. Simpson	(N.Z.)	J. K. Andrews 7-5 6-4 6-4	B. E. Gottfried⑨ 8-6 7-9 2-6 6-4 6-2	
86	R. Gullikson	(U.S.A.)			
87	J. K. Andrews	(U.S.A.)	B. E. Gottfried⑨ 6-3 6-2 9-7		
88	B. E. Gottfried⑨	(U.S.A.)			
89	J. Fassbender	(G.)	J. Delaney 6-2 3-6 6-8	C. S. Dibley 7-5 8-6	B. Borg④ 6-4 6-4
90	J. Delaney	(U.S.A.)			
91	C. S. Dibley	(A.)	C. S. Dibley 6-2 6-3 8-6		
92	P. C. Kronk	(A.)			
93	F. D. McMillan	(S.A.)	M. C. Riessen 6-3 6-3 8-6	B. Borg④ 6-2 6-2 6-4	
94	M. C. Riessen	(U.S.A.)			
95	D. A. Lloyd	(G.B.)	B. Borg④ 6-3 6-3 6-1		
96	B. Borg④	(SW.)			
97	B. M. Bertram	(S.A.)	N. Pilic 8-9 9-8	N. Pilic 8-9 9-8 6-3 5-7 6-4	N. Pilic 3-6 6-4 6-3
98	N. Pilic	(YU.)			
99	V. Pecci	(PA.)	V. Pecci 6-3 6-3 6-4...		
100	P. J. Cramer	(S.A.)			
101	R. A. Lewis	(G.B.)	R. A. Lewis 6-4 2-6 6-2	R. A. Lewis 3-6 9-7 9-8 9-8	
102	P. Proisy	(F.)			
103	B. Teacher	(U.S.A.)	B. Teacher 1-6 8-6 6-4 9-7 9-8		
104	J. F. Holladay	(U.S.A.)			
105	J. ... Smith	(G.B.)	C. Kirmayr 6-3 9-7 5-7 6-2	C. Kirmayr 8-6 6-3 6-3	R. Tanner⑦ 8-9 6-3 6-2
106	C. Kirmayr	(BR.)			
107	C. J. Mottram	(G.B.)	H. J. Pohmann 9-8 6-1 rtd.		
108	H. J. Pohmann	(G.)			
109	K. Hirai	(J.)	K. Hirai 6-3 6-4 6-0...	R. Tanner⑦ 6-3 6-4 9-7	
110	V. Borisov	(U.S.S.R.)			
111	C. M. Robinson	(G.B.)	R. Tanner⑦ 8-6 7-5 6-4		
112	R. Tanner⑦	(U.S.A.)			
113	T. I. Kakulia	(U.S.S.R.)	T. I. Kakulia 6-1 9-8 6-2	T. I. Kakulia 6-1 6-3 6-4	S. R. Smith⑧ 8-6 3-6 6-1 6-1
114	B. Taroczy	(HU.)			
115	R. W. Drysdale	(G.B.)	E. C. Drysdale 6-2 6-3 6-4		
116	E. C. Drysdale	(S.A.)			
117	G. Battrick	(G.B.)	G. Battrick 6-3 6-3 7-5...	S. R. Smith⑧ 6-0 6-8 6-2 6-3	
118	H. J. Plotz	(G.)			
119	P. Cornejo	(CH.)	S. R. Smith⑧ 6-1 6-2 6-4		
120	S. R. Smith⑧	(U.S.A.)			
121	R. J. Carmichael	(A.)	R. J. Carmichael 4-6 6-2 6-1 4-6 7-5	I. El Shafei 8-6 6-4 6-4	J. S. Connors② 6-4 6-0 6-3
122	R. D. Crealy	(A.)			
123	I. El Shafei	(E.)	I. El Shafei 9-8 6-3 6-4...		
124	I. F. Caujolle	(F.)			
125	S. A. Warboys	(G.B.)	S. A. Warboys 5-7 3-6 6-4 6-3 6-2	J. S. Connors② 6-3 6-2 6-3	
126	J. M. P. Marks	(A.)			
127	A. Zugarelli	(IT.)	J. S. Connors② 6-3 6-2 6-3		
128	J. S. Connors②	(U.S.A.)			

1976 Wimbledon Draw.

Men's Singles

Champion: J. S. Connors①

Final: J. S. Connors① def. J. P. McEnroe

Semifinals:
- J. S. Connors① 7-9 6-2 3-6 6-3 6-3 (def. B. M. Bertram)
- J. P. McEnroe 6-4 3-6 4-6 6-3 6-4 (def. P. C. Dent⑧)

Quarterfinals:
- J. S. Connors① 6-2 7-5 6-4 (def. S. R. Smith⑯)
- B. M. Bertram 6-3 6-2 7-5 (def. K. G. Warwick)
- J. P. McEnroe 7-5 4-6 6-3 6-1 (def. A. Mayer)
- P. C. Dent⑧ 6-3 3-6 9-8 1 6-9 7 (def. T. E. Gullikson)

Round results:
- J. S. Connors① 6-2 7-5 6-4 def. E. C. Drysdale
- S. R. Smith⑯ 6-3 5-7 9-8 7-5 def. O. Parun
- K. G. Warwick 6-4 3-6 6-4 2-6 8-6 def. R. C. Lutz●
- B. M. Bertram 6-4 6-0 6-2 def. P. C. Kronk
- J. P. McEnroe 6-2 6-2 5-7 6-3 def. K. Meiler
- A. Mayer 6-4 9 7 6 4 def. J. Andrew
- P. C. Dent⑧ 8-6 3-6 6 7-5 def. R. J. Moore
- T. E. Gullikson 9 8 6 3 8 9 6 3 def. B. E. Fairlie

No.	Player	Country	R1	R2
1	J. S. Connors①	(U.S.A.)		J. S. Connors① 6-3 6-2 6-4
2	R. A. Lewis	(G.B.)	M. C. Riessen 6-3 1-6 8-6	
3	M. C. Riessen	(U.S.A.)		
4	C. J. Lewis	(N.Z.)		
5	I. Borowiak	(U.S.A.)	B. C. Drysdale 8-9 6-3 7-1	E. C. Drysdale 6-3 6-4 6-3
6	B. C. Drysdale	(S.A.)		
7	J. Grant	(CZ)	M. Estep 6-3 4-6 7-9 6-2	
8	M. Estep	(U.S.A.)		
9	W. Scanlon	(U.S.A.)	R. J. Simpson 6-3 7-5 7-5	O. Parun 9-8 6-3 6-4
10	R. J. Simpson	(N.Z.)		
11	O. Parun	(N.Z.)	O. Parun 8-6 7-5 9-8	
12	G. W. Seewagen	(U.S.A.)		
13	C. M. Pasarell	(U.S.A.)	C. M. Pasarell 6-2 6-1 6-4	S. R. Smith⑯ 6-4 6-2
14	B. Teacher	(U.S.A.)		
15	R. D. Crealy	(A.)	S. R. Smith⑯ 6-4 6-2 6-2	
16	S. R. Smith⑯	(U.S.A.)		
17	R. C. Lutz●	(U.S.A.)	R. C. Lutz● 6-3 8-4 6-3	R. C. Lutz● 5-7 6-3 7-5 6-2
18	B. Mitton	(S.A.)		
19	H. Walike	(U.S.A.)	R. D. Ralston 5-7 6-4 6-2	
20	R. D. Ralston	(U.S.A.)		
21	D. A. Lloyd	(G.B.)	D. A. Lloyd 6-4 3-6 6-3 3-6 6-4	K. G. Warwick 8-6 6-1 6-4
22	R. E. Ycaza	(EC)		
23	K. G. Warwick	(A.)	K. G. Warwick 6-2 6-2 6-3	
24	G. Masters	(A.)		
25	P. C. Kronk	(A.)	P. C. Kronk 7-5 6-3 3-6 1-6 6-4	P. C. Kronk 5-7 6-4 6-8 6-3 6-1
26	F. Delaney	(U.S.A.)		
27	F. Gebert	(G.)	D. Palm 6-3 6-4 6-1	
28	C. S. Dibley	(A.)		
29	B. M. Bertram	(S.A.)	B. M. Bertram 4-6 3-6 2-6 6-3 6-2	B. M. Bertram 6-2 4-6 6-3
30	B. Benavides	(BOL)		
31	B. E. Gottfried⑤	(U.S.A.)	B. E. Gottfried⑤ 6-3 6-4 6-4	
32	B. Tanner⑤	(U.S.A.)		
33	B. Tanner⑤	(U.S.A.)	J. M. Lloyd 3-6 6-4 6-4 8-6	K. Meiler 2-6 3-6 6-2 6-4 9-7
34	J. M. Lloyd	(G.B.)		
35	K. Meiler	(G.)	K. Meiler 7-5 4-6 6-1 7-5	
36	R. J. Hewitt	(S.A.)		
37	J. W. Feaver	(G.B.)	C. Dowdeswell 6-1 2-6 2-6 6-1 6-3	J. P. McEnroe 9-7 6-3 6-1
38	C. Dowdeswell	(RH)		
39	J. P. McEnroe	(U.S.A.)	J. P. McEnroe 6-0 7-5 6-4	
40	I. El Shafei	(E.)		
41	K. B. Walts	(U.S.A.)	K. B. Walts 6-4 9-8 5-7 8-9 8-6	J. Andrew 6-2 6-4
42	J. M. P. Marks	(A.)		
43	J. Andrew	(V.)	J. Andrew 6-4 6-2 6-4	
44	S. W. Carnahan	(U.S.A.)		
45	A. Mayer	(U.S.A.)	A. Mayer 6-2 3-6 6-2 8-9	A. Mayer 8-9 6-0 6-2 6-4
46	D. Joubert	(S.A.)		
47	E. van Dillen	(U.S.A.)	A. Panatta⑧ 6-4 9-8 4-6 6-3	
48	A. Panatta⑧	(IT.)		
49	P. C. Dent⑧	(A.)	P. C. Dent⑧ 6-1 6-2 6-2	P. C. Dent⑧ 2-6 9-8 6-3 4-6 6-4
50	W. C. Lolgren	(U.S.A.)		
51	J. E. Mandarino	(BR)	A. Amritraj 7-5 6-1 6-2	
52	A. Amritraj	(IN.)		
53	A. M. Jarrett	(G.B.)	R. J. Moore 6-3 6-3 6-4	R. J. Moore 6-4 6-3
54	R. I. Moore	(S.A.)		
55	L. Alvarez	(SP.)	L. Alvarez 6-4 4-6 6-3 6-3	
56	B. Tzung	(N.Z.)		
57	B. E. Fairlie	(N.Z.)	B. E. Fairlie 8-9 7-5 8-6 6-4	B. E. Fairlie 8-6 4-6 6-4 6-3
58	V. C. Amaya	(U.S.A.)		
59	M. H. Machette	(U.S.A.)	R. J. Carmichael 4-6 6-3 9-8 6-3	
60	R. J. Carmichael	(A.)		
61	T. E. Gullikson	(U.S.A.)	T. E. Gullikson 6-2 6-4 6-3	T. E. Gullikson 6-3
62	S. Krulevitz	(U.S.A.)		

1977 Wimbledon Draw.

Winner: B. Borg — 3-6, 6-2, 6-1, 5-7, 6-4

Semi-final (this half): B. Borg — 6-4, 3-6, 3-6, 8-6

#	Player	Country	First round
63	P. Fleming	(U.S.A.)	R. Ramirez⑦ 6 4 3-6 6-2
64	R. Ramirez⑦	(M.)	
65	V. Gerulaitis⑧	(U.S.A.)	V. Gerulaitis⑧ 6-1 9-8
66	T. W. Gorman	(U.S.A.)	
67	G. Mayer	(U.S.A.)	G. Mayer 6-4 6-2 6-4
68	J. K. Holladay	(U.S.A.)	
69	J. R. Smith	(G.B.)	J. R. Smith 6-4 6-4 6-2
70	W. P. O. Prinsloo	(S.A.)	
71	H. J. Bunis	(U.S.A.)	H. J. Bunis 8-9 6-4 6-8 9-8 8-6
72	G. E. Reid	(CH.)	
73	H. G. Gildemeister	(CH.)	H. G. Gildemeister 6-8 6-4 6-3
74	B. Prajoux	(CH.)	
75	F. V. McNair	(U.S.A.)	F. V. McNair 8-9 16-14
76	N. Saviano	(U.S.A.)	
77	S. Sorensen	(IRE.)	
78	R. G. Laver	(A.)	R. G. Laver 8-0 6-2
79	R. W. Drysdale	(G.B.)	
80	R. L. Stockton⑨	(U.S.A.)	R. L. Stockton⑨ 6-3 9-8 6-3
81	M. Cox⑯	(G.B.)	M. Cox⑯ 6 4 7-5 8-6
82	K. J. Chappell	(S.A.)	
83	J. G. Alexander	(A.)	J. G. Alexander 6-3 6-4
84	A. H. Lloyd	(G.B.)	
85	R. L. Bohrnstedt	(U.S.A.)	R. L. Bohrnstedt 8-9 9-8
86	A. K. Gardiner	(A.)	
87	P. Dominguez	(F.)	P. Dominguez 6-4 4-6 6-2
88	S. Menon	(IN.)	
89	W. W. Martin	(S.A.)	W. W. Martin 6-4 6-4 6-1
90	D. Schneider	(A.)	
91	R. O. Ruffels	(G.B.)	R. O. Ruffels 7-5 8-6 2-6
92	R. Taylor	(S.A.)	
93	J. M. Yuill	(S.A.)	J. M. Yuill 6-3 6-4 6-3
94	A. Betancur	(COL.)	
95	J. Kodes	(CZ.)	
96	G. Vilas①	(ARG.)	G. Vilas① 9-8 7-5 6-4
97	I. Nastase④	(RU.)	I. Nastase④ 6-2 6-1 6-3
98	T. R. Gullikson	(U.S.A.)	
99	R. E. Montano	(M.)	
100	A. J. Pattison	(U.S.A.)	A. J. Pattison 6-1 6-4 6-4
101	C. Letcher	(U.S.A.)	
102	E. Teltscher	(U.S.A.)	E. Teltscher 6-3 0-6 6-2
103	R. Dupre	(U.S.A.)	
104	T. Smid	(CZ.)	P. Dupre 6-4 6-4 5-7 8-6
105	R. Fisher	(U.S.A.)	
106	C. P. Kachel	(A.)	C. P. Kachel 6-3 6-3 6-4
107	A. J. Stone	(A.)	A. J. Stone 9-8 7-5 6-2
108	C. Kirmayr	(BR.)	
109	T. S. Okker	(NTH.)	T. S. Okker 6-2 6-1
110	R. L. Case	(A.)	
111	S. Docherty	(U.S.A.)	S. Docherty 6-4 4-6 7-5 7-5
112	H. Solomon③	(U.S.A.)	
113	W. Fibak⑪	(POL.)	W. Fibak⑪ 6-3 4-6 4-6 6-2
114	J. Filiol	(CH.)	
115	J. E. Norback	(U.S.A.)	J. E. Norback 6-1 3-6 6-4
116	J. McManus	(U.S.A.)	
117	F. D. McMillan	(S.A.)	F. D. McMillan 6-4 6-4 6-4
118	R. Fassbender	(G.)	
119	C. J. Mottram	(G.B.)	C. J. Mottram 4-6 6-4 6-4 6-2
120	J. S. Hagey	(U.S.A.)	
121	N. Pilic	(YU.)	N. Pilic 9-8 6-3 6-2
122	H. Pfister	(U.S.A.)	
123	V. Amritraj	(IN.)	V. Amritraj 4-6 6-3 7-5
124	S. E. Stewart	(U.S.A.)	
125	M. D. Wayman	(G.B.)	M. R. Edmondson 6-4 8-9 7-5
126	M. R. Edmondson	(A.)	
127	A. Zugarelli	(IT.)	B. Borg② 6-1 6-2 9-7
128	B. Borg②	(SW.)	

Second round:
- V. Gerulaitis⑧ 6-3 6-1 6-1
- J. R. Smith 7-5 1-6 6-4
- F. V. McNair 6-3 6-2 7-5
- R. L. Stockton⑨ 3-6 9-7 6-4 7-5
- M. Cox⑯ 8-6 6-4 7-5
- P. Dominguez 6-2 9-8 6-3
- W. W. Martin 2-6 9-6 8-2 10-8
- G. Vilas① 6-2 3-6 8-6
- I. Nastase④ 3-6 7-5 8-6 6-3
- E. Teltscher w.o.
- A. J. Stone 8-6 6-3
- T. S. Okker 7-5 6-3 7-5
- W. Fibak⑪ 6-0 6-2
- C. J. Mottram 7-5 7-5
- B. Borg② 7-9 6-2 6-4 6-1

Third round:
- V. Gerulaitis⑧ 6-3 8-6 6-4
- R. L. Stockton⑨ 6-4 6-3 6-2
- M. Cox⑯ 6 4 6-1 8-6
- W. W. Martin 6-2 6-2 6-4 6-2
- I. Nastase④ 6-4 6-1 6-3 6-1
- T. S. Okker 2-6 9-8 7-5 6-4
- W. Fibak⑪ 9-8 6-3 3-6 6-2 / 7-5 6-3
- B. Borg②

Fourth round:
- V. Gerulaitis⑧ 6 1 6 4 3 6 6 4
- W. W. Martin 3 6 3 6 4 0 6 9 7
- I. Nastase④ 6 8 6 4 6 4
- B. Borg② 6 0 8 6 6 3

Quarter-final:
- V. Gerulaitis⑧ 6 2 6 2
- B. Borg② 6 4 6 2

Semi-final: B. Borg — 6-4, 3-6, 3-6, 8-6

and strong enough to carry the additional strain that doubles puts on you.

I think I could play good doubles because I return serve well. But I would have to play all the time. Right now, the few times I play in Davis Cup and exhibitions, I may enjoy it, but I have no real confidence, because the angles and strategy are so different. I know I'd be crazy ever to play the doubles at Wimbledon as long as I care about winning the singles.

I think my best Wimbledon tennis was in 1976, when I won without losing a set. I was not supposed to win, so there was no pressure. I just hit away in each match and it seemed impossible to miss. I still didn't have much experience on grass, no really big wins; my serve was still suspect. But I thought I had a chance. First I saw the semis as a definite possibility. Then once I made the finals, I knew it would be difficult even though it was to be against Nastase. I was confident against him usually. But he had been in a Wimbledon final before, and I was worried about his experience. I remember losing the first three games and being scared I wouldn't win a game and be the first person ever to lose a Wimbledon final, 6–0, 6–0, 6–0. Then, after I won a few games, I got loose. I reached the stage in the first set where the score was reasonably close and I hadn't embarrassed myself. I already had done well to get to the finals and now I had nothing to lose. So I started playing well, hitting lines and returning everything with no pressure.

That was also the year Mariana and I became close. She had been staying at another, smaller hotel. A few days before the Championships I asked why she didn't move into Lennart's and my suite at the Grosvenor House. When I first asked Lennart, he wasn't pleased; but he said OK. Mariana moved in the next day, which made me happy and relaxed.

Nineteen seventy-seven was physically the most punishing Wimbledon ever for me. I barely won against Mark Edmondson in a second-round five-setter on the new court 14. The surface was soft, and there was no way we could have any rallies. I was playing OK, but the ball just didn't bounce. Even Ilie Nastase had problems with this court. After he polished off Eliot Teltscher, 6–4, 6–3, 6–1, mobs of teen-agers surrounded him pushing over the barriers and causing serious concern about crowd control and the safety of the alleyways. Nastase had a major role in preventing what could have been a catastrophe by exercising patience and humor with his worshippers. Afterward in the tearoom Nastase asked, "Why do all these little girls like me? I'm thirty-one, married and very ugly."

I had some rough patches with Nikki Pilic's savage left-handed serve but won, 9–7, 7–5, 6–3 in the third round. The next test was against Gerulaitis in a semi-final that British TV commentator Dan Maskell called "one of the best matches ever seen on the center court—in the same family as the 1972 Smith-Nastase final." It lasted over three hours, and each time I'd get a tiny lead Vitas would charge to catch up.

For sure I thought I was going to lose when he got a break in the fifth set. He was playing unbelievably, and I got tired, though I think he was too. I remember thinking if I lose it's because this guy has just played too well for too long. The biggest point of the match was when Vitas stayed back on his second serve at 40–30, leading 3–2 in games. Up to that point he had come to net on anything. We had a long rally and finally he came in. I passed him with a backhand down the line. Then I killed him with two lucky top-spin lobs, one that caught him off balance forcing him to hit an awkward overhead wide and the other tricked him totally— he could only watch helplessly from the net as the ball soared over his head. I had broken back.

If I had lost the 1977 final, I think I would have committed suicide. I had 4–0 and 30–40 for 5–0 in the fifth set against Connors. When he came back to 4 all, the feeling I had was unbelievable. I almost started to cry. It's a Wimbledon final, you had the match won, and now you've lost it. I've never had that feeling before or since. Even my five-setters against Edmondson and Gerulaitis were not as harrowing.

I started the Connors match exhausted because of that long semi-final with Gerulaitis. I had been playing Team Tennis with Cleveland and was tired generally from all the traveling. To get up for another day right after Vitas was tough.

Connors is like me. He hates to lose. You always feel the

pressure against Jimmy. He is trying like hell, and it's a great feeling to beat him because you know he has tried so hard on every point. He always puts out his best. I lost the first set 6–3 and won the next two very easily. Then at 4 all in the fourth I had break point for 5–4, my serve to follow for the match. I played a bad point and lost it, and the set 7–5. A poor point does affect me, though I try not to let it. But I do sense the disappointment. After a short while I convince myself that thinking about the past won't help. I can block out the missed point, but sometimes not right away.

Over-all I think officials are pretty good. I get angry over bad calls but over a long match, the standard is OK. I don't lose confidence in the umpires, though I know many players do. The only real solution is to do something electronically with the lines. You know, a secret device is being made in Sweden. There's a court hidden by technicians in a forest in the south of Sweden where all the lines are wired. The umpire has earphones, so he alone can hear when a ball is in or out. At Wimbledon, it's a tradition that you have to be old to be a center-court linesman. And they never change their minds.

When I was ahead 4–0 and a point for 5–0 against Connors in the final set, I remember getting tentative. I guess I wanted Jimmy to lose the point rather than win it myself. I lost depth on my ground strokes and missed far too many first serves. Connors, sensing my hesitation, was suddenly all over the court smacking returns and approaches for winners. His serve had new bite, and quickly he came back to 4 all. But it is far easier to take risks and play boldly when you are behind. As soon as he had caught up, he too lost his daring. He double-faulted on the first point at 4 all and became timid. I won seven of the last eight points. It was the tiredest tennis match I have ever played. After three and a half hours on center court, I doubt that I could have played another game.

Coach Bergelin disagreed, "Borg may appear calm or tired on the surface, but underneath there is still fire. He's tougher mentally and physically than Connors."

Nineteen seventy-eight was a strange final. Jimmy started out so well. That year I had a lot of pressure and was nervous because I had a chance to win Wimbledon three times. Yet at the same time I was more relaxed than the first year I won.

Victor Amaya was my major stumbling point in 1978. I hate playing first rounds. Everything is strange, the courts, the weather, the grounds, the crowds, the scene. It takes almost a week to get used to. There were no bounces and no rallies—and no sunshine; and the temperature was 52 degrees Fahrenheit—for five sets against Amaya. He had me two sets to one, 3–1 and break point on my second serve in the fourth. Here my philosophy of taking chances when you're behind paid off. I cracked a hard serve down the middle, Victor was totally taken by surprise, and he fell apart. I won the last two sets, 6–3, 6–3.

Unlike any other major tournament, you can't ever practice on Wimbledon's center court. At the French, U. S., and Australian Open, you can always hit a few on the stadium court to get used to the surroundings. But at Wimbledon you can't hit one single ball on the center. I'm used to practicing on the same or a similar court before I play my first-round match—that's why first rounds are so difficult for me at Wimbledon. Also, the grass is slick and soft the first week. By the second Monday, the turf is worn down and playing more like a clay court.

In 1978 I wasn't that confident that I would win against Connors; still, I was not really worried that I would lose. One thing helped. Jimmy can't hurt me on his serve. His first serve doesn't go in as often as during his big year, 1974, and it's not as hard. If you serve well on grass, you can win easy points, stupid points, free points because uneven bounces make the ball difficult to return. Also when I have to volley I know the grass will help, because the ball won't sit up. A short bad volley is a good one on grass.

The scores, 6–2, 6–2, 6–3, say I destroyed Jimmy. He won the first two games and only five afterward, but both of us played good tennis. It's just that I won every single big point. And for the first time I came to net much of the time, missing only a single volley in the entire match.

Men's Singles

First Round	Second Round	Third Round	Fourth Round	Fifth Round	Semi-Finals	Final
B. Borg① ......(SW.)	B. Borg① 8-9 6-1 1-6	B. Borg① 6-2 6-2 6-4	B. Borg① 6-2 6-8 6-4 6-4	B. Borg① 6-2 6-4 8-6	Borg 7-5, 6-4, 6-3	Borg 6-4, 6-4, 6-4
V. C. Amaya ......(U.S.A.)						
C. Roger-Vasselin ......(F.)	P. McNamara 8-6 6-3 5-7 6-3					
P. McNamara ......(A.)						
J. Fillol ......(CH.)	J. Fillol 6-2 6-1 2-0 rtd.	J. Fillol 6-3 6-3 6-2				
J. Kodes ......(CZ.)						
K. W. Drysdale ......(G.B.)	R. W. Drysdale 2-6 2-6 6-1					
J. Hrebec ......(CZ.)						
O. Bengtson ......(SW.)	O. Bengtson 6-4 6-4 7-5	G. Masters 6-0 6-8 9-8 6-4	G. Masters 7-5 6-3 6-1			
F. S. Stolle ......(A.)						
W. Scanlon ......(U.S.A.)	G. Masters 7-5 6-8 6-3 6-2					
G. Masters ......(A.)						
F. D. McMillan ......(S.A.)	F. D. McMillan 6-1 6-2	F. D. McMillan 9-8 6-3				
K. Fagel ......(U.S.A.)						
D. Palm ......(SW.)	C. J. Mottram● 7-5 6-2					
C. J. Mottram● ......(G.B.)						
W. Fibak● ......(POL.)	W. Fibak● 6-3 7-5 7-5	W. Fibak● 8-6 4-6 6-2 6-4	W. Fibak● 4-6 7-5 6-1 9-7	A. A. Mayer⑨ 6-4 6-2 6-8 1-6 7-5		
J. L. Clerc ......(ARG.)						
J. C. Kriek ......(S.A.)	J. C. Kriek 6-4 7-5 6-3					
T. Wilkison ......(U.S.A.)						
J. G. Paish ......(G.B.)	R. O. Ruffels 6-3 6-4 6-2	T. Moor 7-5 7-5 9-8				
K. O. Ruffels ......(G.B.)						
M. Lara ......(M.)	T. Moor 6-2 6-4 9-8					
T. Moor ......(U.S.A.)						
V. Winitsky ......(U.S.A.)	V. Winitsky 6-1 6-3 4-6	M. C. Riessen 6-3 6-2 9-7	A. A. Mayer⑨ 8-6 7-5 6-3			
B. Manson ......(U.S.A.)						
M. J. Fishbach ......(U.S.A.)	M. C. Riessen 6-1 8-2 6-2					
M. C. Riessen ......(U.S.A.)						
M. R. Edmondson ......(U.S.A.)	M. R. Edmondson 3-6 2-6 6-4	A. A. Mayer⑨ 6-2 4-6 6-2				
M. J. Moore ......(A.)						
T. Sad ......(CZ.)	A. A. Mayer⑨ 7-5 6-4 6-3					
A. A. Mayer⑨ ......(S.A.)						
G. Vilas④ ......(ARG.)	G. Vilas④ 6-4 6-3 6-3	G. Vilas④ 2-6 6-4 6-3	T. S. Okker 6-4 6-2	T. S. Okker 6-1 9-8 6-1	Okker 7-5, 6-1, 2-6, 6-3	
R. Smith ......(U.S.A.)						
J. W. Feaver ......(G.B.)	J. W. Feaver 6-4 6-4 6-4					
M. Bailey ......(U.S.A.)						
O. Parun ......(N.Z.)	T. S. Okker 6-8 6-3 6-2	T. S. Okker 6-2 6-3				
T. S. Okker ......(NTH.)						
Y. Noah ......(F.)	Y. Noah 8-9 3-6 6-2 6-1 10-8					
R. E. Ycaza ......(EC.)						
A. Zugarelli ......(IT.)	A. Zugarelli 7-5 4-6 2-6 6-3	T. Leonard 6-2 6-4 9-8	T. Leonard 4-6 8-6 6-3			
P. Kuchel ......(A.)						
P. McNamee ......(A.)	T. Leonard 6-3 6-4 6-3					
T. Leonard ......(U.S.A.)						
S. Krulevitz ......(U.S.A.)	B. E. Fairlie 6-3 6-3 7-5	B. E. Fairlie 6-3 6-3				
B. E. Fairlie ......(N.Z.)						
S. Docherty ......(U.S.A.)	S. Docherty 5-7 7-5					
A. R. Ashe③ ......(U.S.A.)						
I. Nastase⑦ ......(RU.)	I. Nastase⑦ 6-2 6-2 6-3	I. Nastase⑦ 6-3 6-4 9-7	I. Nastase⑦ 6-3 1-6 6-3	I. Nastase⑦ 2-6 6-4 6-2 6-3		
J. M. Yuill ......(S.A.)						
S. Birner ......(CZ.)	G. Oeleppo 6-3 4-6 6-4 8-6					
G. Oeleppo ......(IT.)						
V. Zednik ......(CZ.)	M. H. Machette 9-7 4-6 6-3	T. R. Gullikson 6-4 6-2				
M. H. Machette ......(U.S.A.)						
R. J. Carmichael ......(A.)	T. R. Gullikson 6-3 6-4 8-6					
T. R. Gullikson ......(U.S.A.)						
J. Granat ......(CZ.)	P. Fleming 9-8 9-8 6-4	F. V. McNair 9-8	R. Tanner⑤ 6-4 6-2			
P. Fleming ......(U.S.A.)						
C. Letcher ......(A.)	F. V. McNair 6-3 7-5 6-4					
F. V. McNair ......(U.S.A.)						
R. G. Giltinan ......(A.)	R. G. Giltinan 6-2 6-1 9-8	R. Tanner⑤ 6-2 6-4				
D. A. Lloyd ......(G.B.)						
I. El Shafei ......(E.)	R. Tanner⑤ 8-9 1-6 9-8 9-7 6-2					
R. Tanner⑤ ......(U.S.A.)						

1978 Wimbledon Draw.

Winner: BORG 6-2, 6-2, 6-3

Final: Connors 9-7, 6-2, 6-1

Semi-finals: Gerulaitis 7-5, 4-6, 9-7, 6-2 — Connors 6-4, 6-4, 6-2

First round / Entrants:

Player	Country
B. E. Gottfried(5)	(U.S.A.)
J. M. Lloyd	(U.S.A.)
B. Teacher	(U.S.A.)
R. C. Lutz	(U.S.A.)
T. Rocavert	(A.)
A. J. Stone	(A.)
M. J. Farrell	(G.B.)
B. Mitton	(S.A.)
J. Simbera	(CZ.)
A. M. Jarrett	(G.B.)
A. J. Pattison	(U.S.A.)
T. E. Gullikson	(U.S.A.)
W. W. Martin	(U.S.A.)
E. J. van Dillen	(U.S.A.)
J. P. McEnroe(8)	(U.S.A.)
R. L. Stockton(8)	(U.S.A.)
J. M. P. Marks	(A.)
N. Saviano	(U.S.A.)
C. Bradnam	(G.B.)
H. Pfister	(U.S.A.)
A. Filiol	(CH.)
D. Carter	(A.)
R. A. Lewis	(G.B.)
M. D. Wayman	(G.B.)
S. E. Stewart	(U.S.A.)
R. Fisher	(U.S.A.)
J. F. Caujolle	(F.)
J. Royappa	(IN.)
H. Gunthardt	(SWZ.)
V. Gerulaitis(3)	(U.S.A.)
R. Ramirez(7)	(M.)
C. S. Dibley	(A.)
R. D. Crealy	(A.)
D. Schneider	(S.A.)
I. Tiriac	(RU.)
R. J. Frawley	(A.)
E. Deblicker	(F.)
R. Sanders	(NTH.)
P. C. Dent	(A.)
A. D. Roche	(A.)
V. Amritraj	(IN.)
C. Kirmayr	(BR.)
R. L. Case	(A.)
B. Prajoux	(CH.)
D. H. Collings	(A.)
J. D. Newcombe(16)	(A.)
J. G. Alexander(9)	(A.)
V. Pecci	(PA.)
J. R. Smith	(G.B.)
Anand Amritraj	(IN.)
G. Hardie	(U.S.A.)
R. A. J. Hewitt	(S.A.)
C. Dowdeswell	(G.B.)
R. Taylor	(G.B.)
R. Lewis	(N.Z.)
T. W. Gorman	(U.S.A.)
M. Cox	(G.B.)
J. James	(A.)
K. G. Warwick	(A.)
R. J. Simpson	(N.Z.)
J. S. Connors(2)	(U.S.A.)

Second round:
- B. E. Gottfried(5) 6-1 6-8 8-6 6-4
- B. Teacher 6-4 4-3 6-1
- A. J. Stone 6-1 6-4 6-4
- B. Mitton 6-1 5-7 6-1 6-4
- J. Simbera 7-5 8-6 3-6 6-3
- T. E. Gullikson 6-4 3-6 6-1 6-0
- W. W. Martin 5-7 6-4 6-4
- E. J. van Dillen 7-5 1-6 8-9 6-2 9-8
- N. Saviano 6-4 6-2 3-6 6-1
- H. Pfister 6-1 6-1 6-2
- D. Carter 8-6 6-4 9-8
- S. E. Stewart 6-4 9-8 6-3
- R. Fisher 6-3 6-3 6-1
- J. Royappa 2-6 6-3 6-2 6-2
- V. Gerulaitis(3) 4-6 6-1
- R. Ramirez(7) 9-7 9-8 6-3
- D. Schneider 6-2 6-4 9-8
- R. J. Frawley 3-6 6-3 6-4
- E. Deblicker 6-2 8-9 6-3
- P. C. Dent 6-4 7-5 4-6 7-5
- V. Amritraj 6-1 6-3 9-8
- R. L. Case 7-5 4-6 7-9 6-1
- J. D. Newcombe(16) 4-6 7-5
- J. G. Alexander(9) 7-5 4-6 9-8 9-12-10
- R. A. J. Hewitt 3-6 6-3 6-4
- C. Dowdeswell 5-7 6-3 6-4 4-6 6-2
- T. W. Gorman 0-6 6-2 6-2 7-5 6-3
- M. Cox 6-4 3-6 6-4 6-0
- K. G. Warwick 7-5 0-6 2-6 6-4 8-6
- J. S. Connors(2) 6-1

Third round:
- B. E. Gottfried(5) 6-2 7-5 6-3
- A. J. Stone 6-1 2-6 6-8 6-1 10-8
- T. E. Gullikson 6-2 6-3 6-4
- W. W. Martin 5-7 6-8 6-4 7-5
- N. Saviano 6-2 6-3
- H. Pfister 6-3 6-4 9-8
- S. E. Stewart 6-4 9-7 9-7
- V. Gerulaitis(3) 6-3 7-5 6-2
- R. Ramirez(7) 6-1 6-0 6-2
- R. J. Frawley 7-9 6-0 6-0 6-3
- P. C. Dent 3-6 6-3 4-6 7-5
- J. D. Newcombe(16) 6-4 6-2 9-8
- J. G. Alexander(9) 5-7 6-3 7-5 6-2
- R. A. J. Hewitt 6-4 4-6 2-6 6-4
- T. W. Gorman 4-6 8-6 8-6 7-5
- J. S. Connors(2) 6-3 7-5 2-6 6-4

Fourth round:
- B. E. Gottfried(5) 6-8 9-7 6-2 6-1
- T. E. Gullikson 6-3 9-7 7-5
- H. Pfister 9-7 8-9 6-2 6-2
- V. Gerulaitis(3) 9-8 6-0 6-2
- R. Ramirez(7) 6-4 7-5 6-3
- J. D. Newcombe(16) 6-1 1-6 6-4 6-4
- J. G. Alexander(9) 8-6 rtd.
- J. S. Connors(2) 6-4 8-6 8-9 6-3

Quarter-finals:
- B. E. Gottfried(5) 6-2 6-4 6-2
- V. Gerulaitis(3) 6-3 3-6 6-2 6-3
- R. Ramirez(7) 6-2 9-8 6-3
- J. S. Connors(2) 6-2 6-2 6-4

Connors and I give traditional bows to the Royal Box after my victory in the 1978 Wimbledon Final. Even without the scoreboard, Jimmy's expression tells the story.

Here I am with Fred Perry, Wimbledon Champion 1934–36, whose record I broke with my fourth Wimbledon title in 1979.

Fred Perry, the last player to win three Wimbledons in a row and never one known to be kind about the achievements of the game's modern men, said to the press after Borg had tied his record. "No player in history could have lived on center court with Bjorn today. Connors is a great player but he got steamrolled."

At Wimbledon, the post-match interveiws are taped, edited, and typed for distribution to those members of the press who were watching other matches. The following are the transcripts round by round of Borg's record-breaking 1979 Wimbledon.

WIMBLEDON—First Round
Monday 25 June 1979

Bjorn Borg versus Tom Gorman.　　*Borg won:* 3–6, 6–4, 7–5, 6–1
Duration of match: 2 hrs. 6 minutes.

It was the same sort of match as last year against Amaya. This time it was four sets; last year it was five. If Gorman had been lucky he could have won in three straight sets. When I was down 15–40 in the first game of the second set, it was important to win that game. At the start Gorman served well but I returned better as the match went on. I was nervous and tight, but that was because it was the first match. It was a bit difficult to move on the wet court, but after the rain totally stopped it was much better.

There was some controversy after one of my backhands zoomed crazily off the frame for a winner in what three years ago would have been called an illegal double hit. But the rule now is that as long as the stroke is one continuous motion and not "carried" on purpose, the double hit is permitted.

The first couple of rounds are most difficult, for everyone has to get used to the grass, the balls and other things. I don't think I played very well today, but I was satisfied to win. I have been practicing four to five hours each day. I worked hard and felt in good shape.

THE GENTLEMEN'S SINGLES CHAMPIONSHIP

No.	Player	Country
1	B. Borg①	(SW.)
2	T. W. Gorman	(U.S.A.)
3	M. R. Edmondson	(A.)
4	V. Amritraj	(IN.)
5	H. Pfister	(U.S.A.)
6	J. Kodes	(CZ.)
7	P. Fillol	(CH.)
8	P. Fleming	(U.S.A.)
9	D. Schneider	(S.A.)
10	R. J. Carmichael	(A.)
11	B. Teacher	(U.S.A.)
12	C. S. Dibley	(A.)
13	P. C. Kronk	(A.)
14	J. Borowiak	(U.S.A.)
15	A. M. Jarrett	(G.B.)
16	B. E. Gottfried⑦	(U.S.A.)
17	J. G. Alexander⑧	(U.S.A.)
18	J. L. Stockton	(U.S.A.)
19	H. Gu$\cdot$nthardt	(SWZ.)
20	H. Mitton	(S.A.)
21	D. A. Lloyd	(G.B.)
22	O. Parun	(N.Z.)
23	G. Mayer	(U.S.A.)
24	V. C. Amaya	(U.S.A.)
25	T. S. Okker	(NTH.)
26	R. Guedes	(BR.)
27	E. C. Drysdale	(S.A.)
28	J. R. Austin	(U.S.A.)
29	T. Wilkison	(U.S.A.)
30	N. K. Phillips	(A.)
31	G. Taylor	(G.B.)
32	G. Vilas④	(ARG.)
33	J. S. Connors②	(U.S.A.)
34	J. F. Caujolle	(F.)
35	U. Eriksson	(SW.)
36	M. C. Riessen	(U.S.A.)
37	P. C. Krick	(S.A.)
38	P. Feigl	(AU.)
39	J. Fillol	(CH.)
40	J. E. Norback	(SW.)
41	K. Crawford	(U.S.A.)
42	B. Taroczy	(HU.)
43	M. Cox	(G.B.)
44	B. Meier	(G.)
45	J. A. Cortes	(COL.)
46	G. Moretton	(F.)
47	K. J. Moore	(S.A.)
48	M. Orantes⑥	(SP.)
49	C. Barazzutti⑤	(IT.)
50	A. J. Pattison	(U.S.A.)
51	J. B. Fitzgerald	(A.)
52	C. Dowdeswell	(SWZ.)
53	F. Gonzalez	(U.S.A.)
54	B. Bertram	(G.B.)
55	R. W. Drysdale	(G.B.)
56	W. Scanlon	(U.S.A.)
57	B. Drewett	(A.)
58	J. M. P. Marks	(A.)
59	V. E. Iskersky	(U.S.A.)
60	J. James	(U.S.A.)
61	R. Fisher	(A.)
62	P. C. Dent	(A.)

First round

- B. Borg① 3-6 6-4 7-5 6-1
- V. Amritraj 6-7 4-6 8-2 6-2
- H. Pfister 6-3 3-6 7-6
- P. Fleming 3-6 6-3 6-4
- D. Schneider 6-4 7-6 6-1
- B. Teacher 6-4 3-6 6-3 7-5
- J. Borowiak 6-2 6-2 6-4
- B. E. Gottfried⑦ 6-2 7-6 6-1
- J. G. Alexander⑧ 6-1 7-6 6-2
- H. Gu`nthardt 4-6 6-1 6-3
- O. Parun 6-2 4-6 7-5 6-3
- G. Mayer 3-6 6-3 6-4 7-5
- T. S. Okker 6-1 7-5 6-1
- J. R. Austin 6-2 7-6 6-3
- T. Wilkison 6-2 6-2 6-2
- G. Vilas④ 6-3 6-2 6-4
- J. S. Connors② 6-2 6-7 7-5 6-3
- M. C. Riessen 6-3 6-4 7-5
- J. C. Krick 4-6 6-3 6-3 6-0
- J. E. Norback 7-5 6-1 3-6 6-3
- B. Taroczy 6-2 6-2 6-4
- M. Cox 7-5 5-6 3-6 6-3
- G. Moretton 7-5 5-7 6-7 6-2 1-0 rtd.
- M. Orantes⑥ 7-6 4-6 7-6 6-1
- A. J. Pattison 6-3 4-6 4-5
- C. Dowdeswell 6-4 6-7 7-6 6-2
- F. Gonzalez 4-6 6-2 6-2
- W. Scanlon 6-3 6-3 7-5
- B. Drewett 7-5 2-6 7-6 6-2
- V. Pecci③ 6-4 6-7 7-6

Second round

- B. Borg① 2-6 6-4 4-6 7-6 6-2
- H. Pfister 6-1 3-6 6-4
- B. Teacher 6-4 7-6 6-4
- B. E. Gottfried⑦ 7-6 6-4
- J. G. Alexander⑧ 6-3 3-6 5-7 6-3 6-2
- G. Mayer 6-4 6-1 6-2
- T. S. Okker 6-4 3-6 6-2
- T. Wilkison 5-7 7-6 6-2
- J. S. Connors② 6-7 6-3 7-6 6-0
- J. C. Kriek 6-1 6-3 6-1
- M. Cox 6-4 4-6 6-3 7-6
- G. Moretton 3-6 7-6 7-6
- A. J. Pattison 6-3 6-4 0-6
- W. Scanlon 7-6 4-6 6-4 6-2
- B. Drewett 4-6 7-6 7-6 6-4

Third round

- B. Borg① 6-1 6-3
- B. Teacher 6-3 7-5 5-7 6-3
- G. Mayer 6-4 6-4
- T. S. Okker 7-5 6-4
- J. S. Connors② 6-4 6-1 7-6
- M. Cox 3-6 6-7 6-1 7-6 7-5
- W. Scanlon 7-6 4-6 6-4 6-2
- B. Drewett 4-6 7-6 7-6 6-4

Fourth round

- B. Borg① 6-4 5-7 6-4 7-5
- T. S. Okker 7-6 5-7 6-4 6-4
- J. S. Connors② 6-2 6-1 6-1
- W. Scanlon 6-4 6-4 6-7 7-5

Quarter-finals

- B. Borg① 6-2 6-1 6-3
- J. S. Connors② 6-3 4-6 7-6 6-4

Semi-finals

- B. Borg① 6-2 6-1 6-3
- J. S. Connors② 6-3 4-6 7-6 6-4

Final

B. Borg① 6-2 6-3 6-2

R. Tanner①
6-3 7-6 6-3

P. Dupre
3-6 6-4
6-4
6-7 6-3

R. Tanner
6-1 6-4
6-7 6-2

A. Panatta   7-6
6-3 7-6

P. Dupre   3-6
7-5 4-6 6-4 8-6

R. Tanner①   6-7
7-6 6-4 6-1

T. E. Gullikson⑤
6-4 6-2 6-4

A. Panatta   7-6
7-6 7-6

A. A. Mayer   6-7
7-5 7-6 6-2

R. C. Lutz   6-7
6-4 6-3 6-2

P. Dupre   7-5
1-6 6-3 6-1

R. Tanner①   6-4
7-5 7-6

R. L. Case   6-7
7-6 6-3 7-5

J. L. Clerc⑨   6-7
7-6 6-3 7-5

T. E. Gullikson⑤
6-0 6-4 6-1

J. P. McEnroe②
6-4 6-2 6-4

No.	Player		1st round	2nd round
63	S. E. Stewart	(U.S.A.)		
64	V. Pecci①	(PA.)	V. Pecci① 7-5 6-2 6-3	
65	A. R. Ashe⑦	(U.S.A.)		
66	C. P. Kachel	(G.B.)	C. P. Kachel 6-4 7-6 6-3	
67	J. M. Lloyd	(G.B.)		O. Bengtson 7-5
68	O. Bengtson	(SW.)	O. Bengtson 6-3 0-6 6-7 6-4	6-3 6-4 6-1
69	A. K. Gardner	(A.)		
70	J. R. Smith	(G.B.)	J. R. Smith 1-6 6-4 6-2 6-4	
71	A. Panatta	(IT.)		A. Panatta 2-6 6-2
72	A. Gimenez	(SP.)	A. Panatta 6-3 6-3 6-4	6-7 7-5 6-3
73	A. A. Mayer	(U.S.A.)		
74	C. M. Pasarell	(U.S.A.)	A. A. Mayer 6-1 6-7 6-3	A. A. Mayer 6-3
75	J. Andrew	(V.)		7-6 4-6 7-6
76	R. Ramirez	(M.)	R. Ramirez 6-2 6-3 6-1	
77	I. El Shafei	(E.)		J. Sadri 6-3 5-7
78	J. Sadri	(U.S.A.)	J. Sadri 3-6 6-3 7-6 7-6	6-4 7-5
79	J. M. Yuill	(SP.)		
80	J. Higueras④	(SP.)	J. Higueras④ 6-2 7-5 5-7 3-6 6-4	
81	W. Fibak⑥	(POL.)		B. Manson 7-6 4-6
82	B. Manson	(U.S.A.)	B. Manson 4-6 6-7 9-7	6-4 6-4
83	F. Buehning	(U.S.A.)		
84	R. Meyer	(U.S.A.)	F. Buehning 6-3 6-4 6-4	
85	R. C. Lutz	(U.S.A.)		R. C. Lutz 6-7
86	C. Groins	(EC.)	R. C. Lutz 6-3 6-2 6-2	6-4 6-3 6-2
87	R. E. Ycaza	(EC.)		
88	D. P. Whyte	(F.)	R. E. Ycaza 6-4 1-6 6-2	
89	Y. Noah	(IN.)		Y. Noah 6-3 6-4
90	R. Krishnan	(U.S.A.)	Y. Noah 7-6 6-3 7-5	7-5
91	N. Saviano	(U.S.A.)		
92	R. Fagel	(BR.)	N. Saviano 6-0 6-1 6-2	
93	C. kirmayr	(G.B.)		P. Dupre 4-6 7-6
94	J. W. Feaver	(U.S.A.)	C. kirmayr 6-1 4-6 6-3 6-3	6-3 6-4
95	P. Dupre	(U.S.A.)		
96	V. Gerulaitis④	(U.S.A.)	P. Dupre 7-6 6-3 6-3	
97	R. Tanner①	(U.S.A.)		R. Tanner① 6-1
98	V. Winitsky	(A.)	R. Tanner① 6-1 6-4 6-4	7-6 6-4
99	P. McNamara	(CZ.)		
100	A. Leudi	(U.S.A.)	P. McNamara 6-3 6-2 6-3	
101	P. Portes	(U.S.A.)		R. L. Case 6-2 6-1
102	E. Taygan	(ARG.)	P. Portes 1-6 6-4 6-4 6-4	7-5
103	W. W. Martin	(U.S.A.)		
104	R. L. Case	(BR.)	R. L. Case 7-5 6-7 6-4 6-2	
105	C. Motta	(UR.)		S. R. Smith 6-3
106	J. L. Damiani	(A.)	J. L. Damiani 7-5 6-3 6-4	6 2 7-6
107	D. Carter	(U.S.A.)		
108	S. R. Smith	(SP.)	S. R. Smith 6-1 2 6-4 6-1	
109	A. Munoz	(U.S.A.)		J. L. Clerc⑨ 6-1
110	K. G. Giltinan	(ARG.)	A. Munoz 7-6 6-3 3-6 7-5	6-3 6-4
111	J. L. Clerc⑨	(U.S.A.)		
112	T. E. Gullikson⑤	(U.S.A.)	J. L. Clerc⑨ 6-4 4-6 6-4 6-4	
113	M. Cahill	(RH.)		T. E. Gullikson⑤ 7-5 6-7 6-2 6-4
114	H. Ismail	(A.)	T. E. Gullikson⑤ 6-4 6-2 6-2	
115	T. Snid	(CZ.)		
116	K. G. Warwick	(A.)	T. Snid 7-5 7-6 6-2	
117	C. Letcher	(A.)		C. Letcher 6-1 3-6
118	P. Dominguez	(F.)	C. Letcher 7-6 6-1 2-6 7-6	6-3 6-4
119	P. Hutka	(CZ.)		
120	Anand Amritraj	(IN.)	P. Dominguez 6-3 6-3 6-4	
121	A. Maurer	(G.B.)		T. R. Gullikson 6-1 6-4 6-4
122	P. Stolzl	(A.)	A. Maurer 6-3 7-6 7-6	
123	T. K. Gullikson	(CZ.)		
124	K. A. Lewis	(U.S.A.)	T. R. Gullikson 4-6 6-1 3 6-1	
125	C. J. Mottram	(G.B.)		J. P. McEnroe② 6-1 6-4 6-4
126	T. Floor	(U.S.A.)	C. J. Mottram 6-4 6-3 7-5	
127	J. P. McEnroe②	(U.S.A.)	J. P. McEnroe② 7-5 6-1	6-7 6-2 7-6 6-2

1979 Wimbledon Draw.

Bjorn Borg versus Vijay Amritraj. *Borg won:* 2–6, 6–4, 4–6, 7–6, 6–2
Duration of match: 2 hrs. 46 minutes.

I felt I had lost the match for sure at 1–3 and also at 0–40 two–three, fourth set. I was relieved to win that set in the tie-breaker and by then was playing well. Vijay became very nervous in the tie break and made two weak shots. He was especially good when ahead and winning. It was almost exactly the same as last year against Amaya, when I was 3–1 down in the fourth set. But I didn't think about last year. I have been down like this before. I am more relaxed when I'm behind and go all out to make winners. Some of the time I do it. I was not nervous at all. Still, there's no way I can keep winning. I have to lose sometimes. No one can win every single match in every single tournament.

Today's game was even closer than against Amaya last year. I've had two tight matches so far and now face Pfister. I've had service problems, but I'm not worried. It can come right any day. I pulled something in my leg against Gorman, but I hope it will be better with a day's rest tomorrow. I have played Pfister twice before and won twice; they were both tight.

This is the toughest draw I've ever had at Wimbledon. I know Pfister likes to play on grass, and he must have played very well to beat Fleming in four sets. He has a big serve, but I am confident of being able to return it if I play well.

WIMBLEDON—Third Round
Friday 29 June 1979

Bjorn Borg versus Hank Pfister. *Borg won:* 6–4, 6–1, 6–3
Duration of match: 1 hour 12 minutes

I didn't feel my injury much today except when I had to reach wide on the forehand or backhand. I pulled a hamstring at the back of my left thigh, but if it is like this for my next match, I'll be satisfied. Whatever happens, if I am going to lose, it will be on the tennis court—not off it. I have been having ice treatment on the injury every day, also ultrasonic and cream massage.

Before today's match I had some hot stuff rubbed on. Yesterday I rested as much as possible and just had one hour hitting. I have not been pretending about my injury. The treatment I have had has made a difference and I am just going to see how I feel tomorrow.

The doctor says the best treatment is rest. I am not going to have any injections. I was a little scared at the beginning, not knowing how my injury would react, but I felt better and better as the game went on. My return of serve was very good today and it was my best match against Pfister so far. He missed many first serves and he has played better. Even if I lose this year I will come back to Wimbledon and play next year.

WIMBLEDON—Round of 16
Saturday 30 June 1979

Bjorn Borg versus Brian Teacher.   *Borg won:* 6–4, 5–7, 6–4, 7–5
Duration of match: 2 hours 29 minutes.

In a sense, I was ready for Teacher, because he played exactly the way Pfister did in the last round. Big serve, charge the net. Even on my serve he tried to get to the net all the time. I was worried. There weren't many rallies. It was very windy on court 1 today making it difficult to control the ball. Besides you never know how well he is going to do his thing. If he does it perfectly I'm out of the tournament. But I started to play consistently in the Pfister match so I had confidence for Teacher. I've finally gotten used to the conditions, the crowds and the weather.

This match was very, very close. It was one set all and it could go either way in the third set. I did win that one, but the fourth was even trickier. He hit a lot of first serves in; I was returning solidly and still never came close to breaking serve until the end. He had a lot of chances to break me and win that last set.

For me, I was very aggressive, mixing it up by serving and volleying, rallying a few balls and then following an approach to net.

I felt I had to come in more because if I didn't, he would. It was a sort of race to see who could get to net first.

WIMBLEDON—Quarter-finals
Tuesday 3 July 1979

Bjorn Borg versus Tom Okker.   *Borg won:* 6–2, 6–1, 6–3
Duration of match: 1 hour 7 minutes

This was probably my simplest quarter-final ever at Wimbledon. Probably not my best. Tom didn't play well and missed a lot of easy volleys. I feel I am playing well. I am still having treatment on my leg but it hasn't bothered me for the last two matches, and it doesn't matter if I play a long match or a 67-minute one like this. I don't feel in trouble. I believe Connors should have been seeded number 2, and it's a pity to meet Connors in the semi-final. Still, there are some good guys in the lower half, and to reach the final anyone has to play well. At the moment Connors is in good form and has improved a lot, and he is now playing with a lot of confidence and hitting the ball hard and deep. I always believe I am going to win, but against Connors I never know.

There is no way that I can play below my best and win. Tomorrow I will practice for a couple of hours and the rest of the time I will relax and get myself ready for Thursday. It's good to have a day off after a tough match, but like all players I prefer to play everyday.

It was more exciting for me in 1976 than it is for me now, for I never dreamed I could win then. Now everything is working out well. I am completely satisfied, except possibly for my first serve. Little bothers me on court. Much of the rest time I spend in bed.

There is a little more pressure on Connors now against me, for I have been winning lately. Earlier he was beating me more often, and I had the pressure.

WIMBLEDON—Semi-final
Thursday 5 July 1979

Bjorn Borg versus Jimmy Connors.   *Borg won:* 6–2, 6–3, 6–2
Duration of match: 1 hour 16 minutes

I expected a much tougher match, because I did not think I would play so well today. Also Jimmy was below his best. I played as well as I did in the final last year. Jimmy didn't say anything to me after the game. He's probably in a bad temper. I would be too, if I lost. Obviously, we are going to play many more matches against each other, and I feel very confident now. He beat me seven of the first eight times we played starting in 1973, but this has changed. I have won eight of the last eleven. I am hitting my ground strokes better. Earlier in my career I played more soft balls, and he put pressure on me. Now I am hitting through the ball and getting better depth on both sides. In the early days, he was able to come in, but now he has to stay back.

Today, Jimmy missed a lot of first serves. In last year's final he did the same thing. I served well, especially in the first two sets. I have to, because he returns so well. This is the first match in the tournament that I have served well. He played a very good game when he broke my serve at the start of the third set, but I was still feeling good.

To me, Connors is just another player. I like him as a person—I'm just not very close to him. I knew before the tournament began that the first week would be difficult. In the last three years I started playing better by the quarterfinals. It is the same this year. I feel happy about Saturday's final, whomever I play. I know some felt that the match with Connors was virtually the final, but Tanner could be more difficult for me. There are two things which might get better: my serve and my volley. I still get the same thrill and excitement about winning. I always want to win a big tournament. I have no idea why Jimmy leaves the ground so quickly after the matches and doesn't turn up at press conferences. I feel that if I don't go to them I might get a bad press the next day.

PRESS QUESTION: How would you play against yourself?
BORG: I have no idea. I wouldn't tell you anyhow.

WIMBLEDON—Final
Saturday 7 July 1979

Roscoe Tanner versus Bjorn Borg.　*Borg won:* 6–7, 6–1, 3–6, 6–3, 6–4
Duration of match: 2 hours 50 minutes

TANNER INTERVIEW

"If I had won that last point it would have meant four points in a row for me, but the ball kicked a bit. It was not a very bad bounce, but I missed it and the title was his. My coach, Dennis Ralston, told me during the match to keep working at him, and I had to take some chances on his serve to avoid being crowded out. You have to take chances against Bjorn, because he is so much better than anyone else. You have to keep him out of his groove and rhythm. I felt in spots that I made errors that could have been avoided, and he jumped on my second serve too often. At no time did I feel nervous or tense about anything. I was just going for my shots. There was no reason for nerves, for there was no pressure on me and I was keyed up to win. Still, being in the final is not all that bad. I wasn't aware of the crowd noises, which probably meant that I concentrated more. I think the noise implied that they were enjoying a good match.

"I was not tired in any way at the end, although during the match I was a little weary after certain points. He makes you work so hard, and some of his high returns mean a lot of stretching. His serve seemed to be getting weaker toward the end. I served a pretty good match, even though I missed some. You have got to concede that he will occasionally break you—he is such a good player.

"Tomorrow I will probably start remembering all those chances I had of winning. I have to think of ways to improve on my errors, even though I bothered him a lot today. The most important period of the match was when I led 15–40 on his serve at 3–4 down in the final set. I had a great chance of making it 4–4, and when you come down to it just one or two points made all the difference. Dennis had written down some strategy, and during a difficult part of the match I pulled out the piece of paper, read it, started all over again and won the next three games. For part of the match Borg seemed rather tentative, especially in the first set, perhaps because he was going for the fourth title. I think I played a good match against a very good player."

BORG'S INTERVIEW

"I can't yet believe I have won Wimbledon for the fourth time. It hasn't sunk in yet. There will be a big celebration eventually, probably for the next three or four days. Today I feel much older than I am. I was unbelievably nervous at the end and almost couldn't hold my racquet when he came back in the last game from 0–40 to deuce. If he had won that game I could never have won the match. In the beginning he was serving very well and winning the big points, but later I started to take the big points. That was after I decided to come in more. I had to put pressure on him and make sure that I got the ball back and he began to make mistakes especially with his volleys.

"It was difficult to get the feel of the ball and the rhythm of my ground strokes because of the tricky wind, and there was no way I could lob in the conditions. I thought I would lose the match for sure when he was ahead two sets to one.

"I never felt in the fight, because the points were over so quickly. He'd ace me or miss. I didn't control anything. Nothing was happening. Nothing worked. A couple of good points or a break can help enormously. When I get that break point I always play it safely. As soon as it was 2 sets all, I thought I had a good chance to win, especially when I broke the first game of the fifth set. He had a lot of chances to break back, and I remember hoping each time that he would miss. I just didn't want the ball to come back.

"When I won for the first time in 1976 I never imagined I could do it four times running. This is the biggest thrill of my life.

"My future goal is to win more big titles and be regarded as the greatest player of all time. I have won twenty-eight matches at Wimbledon and Rod Laver has won thirty-one, so I want to go for that record next year. My next big tournament is the U.S. Open. I will definitely play in it, and I am going to get myself a hundred percent fit. I seemed fated to win all the big points in this tournament, especially today, but there will come the time when I start losing those points. For the last three or four matches I haven't felt any trouble with my left thigh. Only at the start did it trouble me. This was the most difficult of my four finals because of the way Roscoe was serving. It was even harder than my five-set match with Connors. The pressure was on me, for I knew I had to hold my serve, otherwise I would lose. It was very important to break him at the start of the fifth set. I always felt one step behind until I realized I was fully ahead in the fifth. Some people wonder why I stay back, especially on my second serve. Most opponents come to attack it, but I have such good passing shots that I don't mind that. My parents have been here all the tournament, and they have seen me win Wimbledon twice. They were also here in 1977.

"During that last game when I was serving for the match, my mother was watching in the players' guest section, she always eats candy for luck when I play. She spit it out on the floor when I was 40–0 triple match point. I lost three straight points to deuce. She was so nervous she looked for the candy on the floor, found it and popped it back in her mouth. I won the next two points and the match.

"I wasn't praying to my parents as I told the press afterward. I was kidding them. I didn't think about what I was going to do before the last point. I just did it. I'm not religious. I wasn't praying to God either. I was brought up as a Protestant, but I've only been to church once in my life,

114

when I was nine. I was curious that one time, but now I don't think about religion. For sure sometimes I thank God. I believe in something up there, but I don't believe it too. I don't understand it."

To set Borg's record straight, it should be understood that other men have won four straight Wimbledons. William Renshaw won six straight (1881–1886); Reggie F. Doherty won four straight (1897–1900) and his brother H. Laurie Doherty won five in a row (1902–1906); Tony Wilding won four in succession (1910–1913). Wilding was the only one of these early champions who had to play through the entire tournament—and he did it just once—because prior to 1913, the champion was exempt until the Challenge Round just like the format of the Davis Cup before 1974. Rod Laver won Wimbledon four times in a row with a five year gap in between (1961–'62, '68, '69). He didn't play those intervening five years from 1963 through 1967, because pros weren't permitted at Wimbledon until 1968.

CHAPTER

6

Myths

The name Bjorn means "bear" in Swedish. It doesn't fit. Bjorn is a cougar or an eagle, but never so plodding an animal as a bear. His raw speed and acceleration are magnified by their effortlessness. Bjorn never appears to be moving quickly and yet is never out of position. The fact that he rarely has to rush —indeed that he is usually waiting in place long before the ball reaches him—is a striking advantage in stroke preparation.

The Swedish name Borg, on the other hand, means "castle." The perfect description for a player whose defense is impenetrable.

Breaking down myths is as difficult as learning to play tennis left-handed, if you are a right-hander. In the days of the Puritans, when government leaders insisted there were witches and that they were wicked and had to be burned at the stake, they were. Officials had to be right didn't they? So too in tennis, myths have been offered as truth from the "experts" with no room for change.

There is no process where a tennis axiom is tested and tossed out if times have changed, or the "truth" wasn't true in the first place. Countless tennis tips have been passed on from generation to generation without the fresh air of a new theory or examination of the old one.

A prime problem of instruction methods is that the degree of acceptance is often directly related to the reputation of the man teaching, regardless of whether the theory is cockeyed or not. For instance, Hall of Famer Jack Kramer says on the return of serve to hold your racquet with the forehand grip and lean to the right or forehand side. It happens that I do exactly the opposite, holding the backhand grip with the racquet tilting all the way to the backhand.

Another juicy bit of instruction is the advice to hit the ball on the rise. There is a macho urge to strike the ball immediately as it comes off the ground. No one has bothered to add that while hitting on the rise is the ultimate offensive game and dramatic to watch and play, it is low-percentage tennis. It's flashy but won't win consistently. I conclude that the advantages of hitting on the rise—the element of surprise and using your opponent's power— is marginal compared to the risks.

Hitting on the rise is like half-volleying, and I half-volley only because I have to—not because I want to—where my opponent has trapped me out of position and I'm forced to flick at the ball without normal preparation. The advantages of hitting a ball at the top of its bounce, on the other hand, are obvious. The ball's direction will be from a high point to a low point over the net and down into the court rather than the necessary arc from low to high over the net. In addition, you have more time to prepare. Often when I need more time to set up I'll hit the ball as it's falling from the bounce rather than meet it at the top. The added time is important to two-handers whose backswing takes more stages to put together.

That is not to say that some players, like Connors, Fleming and McEnroe, are not sometimes successful in hitting on the rise—particularly on the return of serve when they are going for a one-shot winner. However, the art of hitting on the rise is an imprecise science, not recommended for pros or amateurs. And the concentration required to continually hit on the rise is intense, and that will be tiring in a long match.

CARICATURE BY DAVID LEVINE

If you want me to offer standard advice such as, "take your racquet back, follow through and watch the ball," stop reading. I believe tennis is a game of instinct and common sense rather than proper grips and tedious tips. Not that a youngster doesn't need the fundamentals of stroke production, but once basic guidelines have been laid down and those fundamentals have been burned into a beginner's mind by constant practice, progress from there is a state of mind rather than a state of form.

I have broken nearly every rule recommended by instruction books over the past fifty years. For example, the normal advice on where to stand when returning serve is a *foot* beyond the base line. And, when receiving a second serve, a foot *inside* the base line. Anyone who has seen me play knows I don't do this. Not even close.

COURT POSITION FOR SERVICE RETURN

I position myself as much as ten feet past the base line, and when Roscoe Tanner is serving, I retreat even further back. The reason? I want to get the longest look possible at a hard serve. I need ample time to sight the direction of delivery, then wind up and swing at the ball.

To me, standing at the base line to return serve is for showoffs. Maybe a star can rip off a spectacular winner standing close in, but for every winner struck, he'll miss a dozen. My idea is to get every single service return back so as to pressure the net man into missing. Because my goal is not to hit instant winners, there is no burden on me in returning serve.

Having more time to hit the ball by standing back, plus the no-pressure frame of mind, is a devastating combination. The result is that I end up hitting more outright winners on return of serve than anyone else on the pro tour. Why? The element of surprise.

Most big servers on a fast surface (the grass at Wimbledon, the asphalt at the U.S. Open) are spoiled by having 30 percent of their first serves virtually unreturnable, meaning that 30 percent of the time, the server fires and relaxes. He's lulled by the frequent flubs of players who stand close to the base line. I return every serve. This both annoys and surprises my opponents. Take a look the next tournament I play Roscoe Tanner or Jimmy Connors. Many times they'll serve a ball that is normally an ace against players who return from close in, and, as a result, they relax on their way to net. Midway to the service line they stand up, thinking the return won't come back. But because I'm standing so far away, I have plenty of time to have a solid crack at the ball, which often zips by the unprepared netman.

Why do receivers continue to stand so close in? Mostly because it's macho to face a cannonball next to the barrel. Sort of like the gladiators in the olden days chasing one another with axes or swords at close range.

Two superstars—John McEnroe and Jimmy Connors— have such swift eye-to-brain-to-arm motor control that they actually see the ball coming at them sooner than other players. This phenomenal reflex capacity means that they can stand in the mouth of the cannon, so to speak, and pick up the approaching serve instantly. But even Connors, as he gets older, has started to lose this facility, leaving McEnroe as the only pro with "radar eyes." And McEnroe admits that this ability does not help him at all in returning serve on clay where the ball slows down enough so anyone can return efficiently. You can add the fact that only a few fools try to serve and volley consistently on clay and that eliminates the need to get the jump on the server.

As I say, the macho image has much to do with why pros and amateurs alike dig in close to the base line to return serve. Me? I want my macho moment in the winner's circle rather than for a few isolated points during the match.

My advice works for beginners too. Many amateurs crash their first serve and pitty-pat the second. I say, stand 'way behind the base line to return serve, to give yourself sufficient time to take your racquet back and swing in the unlikely event the crash serve goes in. Even after a first-serve fault, move in only to the point where you have ample time to prepare your stroke. Sure, there is a "give-up" in standing back—an opponent might exploit the angles of a wide serve, but the benefits of having more time, in my opinion, far outweigh the risks.

I'm not alone in my cautious philosophy to wait for the ball far past the base line rather than taking a bolder position smack on it. Guillermo Vilas, who has one of the best clay-court records in recent history, also waits patiently behind the base line. Certainly there are some disadvantages for top pros with this style, the main one being that one has to be in extraordinary shape to execute this defensive game plan successfully. A simple study of court angles shows that you don't have to run so far if you stand in further and move along the diagonals toward the net. In a sense you are cutting the ball off before it becomes a punishing stroke—also, you can use your opponent's pace more effectively if there is less distance between you and the net.

Pancho Gonzalez was one of the first proponents of maneuvering an opponent like a puppet while standing atop the base-line tape. But Pancho hit an underspin backhand and a forehand with only moderate overspin. He was merely waiting for the first opportunity to attack.

My game is different. It is based on patience. Not attack. But my top-spin drives prevent opponents from attacking, because I have enough control to shoot my ground strokes from side to side. If an opponent decides to come to net behind a less-than-perfect approach, he is playing into my strength, dipping passing shots. My game is structured so that I can direct the flow of play with steadiness, yet counterpunch against an aggressive net rusher. In other words, I don't need to take chances with a killer serve and risky full-bore volleys. I win without having the traditional big game —which should be music to everyone's ears, because the serve and volley are the game's two most difficult strokes to master.

In a sense, my design of play is perfect to use against those pros who learn their tennis "by the book." The "book" methods are so routine that the unorthodox player has a big edge when he faces opponents who play according to predictable patterns.

THE RALLY POSITION

Another example of my ignoring standard instruction is my court position *during* a rally. Most "experts" recommend that forehands and backhands should be tackled from approximately two feet behind the base line. I double and sometimes triple that. Why? Because the exchange of ground strokes is a game of attrition. If the base-line style is played properly, no one hits a winner from the back court.

There is no percentage in taking a wild poke at a forehand and hoping it will hit an inch from the side-line corner and scoot for a winner. The odds are stacked against this ploy. First, in aiming for such a small target on court, the chances are you'll miss the attempt outright. Perhaps, by some miracle the ball may land safely, but if you're up against a laser-fast runner like Gerulaitis, he'll track the shot down anyhow, and you'll have to start all over again with the odds doubly loaded against you in having to try to do it all over again.

What is incredible to me about the experts' advice on court positioning is that no distinction is made between slow and fast surfaces. On clay there is no reason not to give yourself plenty of time to run down shot after shot. Standing far behind the base line gives you an opportunity to retrieve, with little fear that your opponent can attack your defensive scurrying.

However, on a fast grass court, the ball tends to skid and stay low, meaning you have to move closer to the base line to scoop up the ball before it bounces twice. On cement or asphalt, ground strokes move with greater velocity than on clay and that requires a position nearer the base line—or else the ball will get out of range too quickly. Also there is a difference between returning a ball that has lost its power and returning a ball—from the same location—that still has plenty of force behind it.

What all this really means is that you should be flexible in your over-all approach to tennis. Don't get trapped by hard-and-fast rules. Just as every player is either taller, shorter, lighter, heavier, stronger or weaker than his opponent, so too do situations and abilities to meet them vary enormously from player to player.

For instance, being two-handed I have a reach that is shorter on the backhand than that of a "one-handed" player. This suggests that I need more time to get into position anywhere on court, and that particularly on the volley I must prepare my approach to net more carefully than Gerulaitis or McEnroe, who both have machine-gun reactions in the forecourt.

But the best example of the need for adaptability is at Wimbledon. Since I have won Wimbledon four times in a row, it is difficult to argue that my tennis is inflexible. This great championship is the only major title on grass, and the pros must adjust to the surface very quickly to survive even a few rounds.

To the true Wimbledon expert, subtle but crucial adjustment must be made between the first and second weeks at Wimbledon. During the first five days of play on the sacred surface at the All England Club, the pitch is lush, green and fast, forcing lightning low bounces—and sometimes no bounces at all. The forceful servers usually have exceptional success the first week, even if the rest of their game is not of the same high standard. I am forced to serve and volley the first week, because I can't afford to let the ball touch the ground, so erratic and rapid is its ricochet.

But by the second week, the grass has become worn down and is brown from the heavy pounding by hundreds of tennis shoes tearing across it. The center court is so packed and solid that it plays very much like clay, my favorite surface. By the quarter-finals, the playing surface is so even and true that I can afford the luxury of staying back on serve and swapping ground strokes. That's my strength.

If my message about the demand for innovation and originality in tennis is still not getting through, it should encourage every novice to know that the first thing I did in tennis was wrong according to all the teaching pros. I used the western forehand grip with a closed racquet face which everyone said was too "wristy" and unreliable. I was told that no modern champion uses the western grip, and there was a lot of advice in the beginning to change to a more accepted approach. Well, it's become my best shot. I'm glad I didn't listen.

The point is that tennis is a highly personalized game. You should do what seems to work for you, rather than be regimented into a lock-step stroke that may be safe and easy to teach, but does not allow your possibly unique talent to emerge.

My backhand is equally unorthodox, double-handed, with a closed racquet face and full of wrist. Because my basic foundation in stroke mechanics is so untraditional, the results are also unusual. For instance, the bedrock of all ground-stroke instruction is to hit the ball with great depth—that is, a ball hitting within a foot of the base line is an excellent shot.

Not the way I play tennis. I believe successful tennis is a game of consistency and taking advantage of proper percentages. Though my passing shots often look spectacular, there is a huge safety factor built in.

SPIN AND DEPTH

If I strike a ball that lands a foot from my opponent's base line, it's an accident, because I'm only aiming for two yards past the service box—for security. My ground strokes are so wristy that it would be impossible to control a ball regularly that's aimed for the base line. I do get depth, however, by using murderous top spin, which carries the ball deep into the back court after the bounce. In this fashion I achieve both depth and margin for error.

It's all possible because of my "crazy" forehand western grip and wristy two-handed backhand, both of which force me to hit with exaggerated overspin. Violent top spin is my trademark, and if I hadn't had the courage to improvise when I was young, and shatter the conventional beliefs about grips and depth, I might still be struggling through the qualifying round at Wimbledon rather than shooting for a string of successive titles.

What I'm saying is for you not to be preoccupied by rigid rules of instruction. Learn your own talents and never be afraid of experimenting with what suits your game best. Remember, I'm trying to teach you to get your mind *and* the ball over the net.

7

Getting the Ball
Over the Net

"Newcombe's or Gonzalez's serve was like an axe—Borg's is
like a rigger's knife, sharp and practical."
                              —*Tennis Week*, February 1980.

I don't believe you teach from a book. You know—"hit the
forehand 20 centimeters in front of your left foot and the
backswing on your backhand at a 60 degree angle from a line
parallel to the net." Nonsense. The books tell you a hundred
different things and then you go out on court and try to remember a hundred rules on how to hit your forehand. Just go
out and hit the stroke and see how it works. Sure there are a
few adjustments you can make, but most of the good advice
you get won't come from a book. You must find out how it
feels for you. If I were teaching a beginner, I'd have him
watch me hit a few. Then I'd put the racquet in his hand and
let him try. Maybe the guy should play with one hand or with
two. You never can say any one thing is right for everyone.
     For example, the classic eastern forehand grip is taught
as the "shake hands grip"—that is, "hold the racquet directly
in front of you with the strings perpendicular to the ground
and then shake hands with the handle." A basic problem with
this suggestion is that everyone is likely to shake hands

Backhand grip

FOUR PHOTOS: E. L. SCOTT

Forehand grip

BJORN BORG

Return-on-serve grip

Continental grip (used for forehand and backhand volley, serve, overhead)

somewhat differently. Try it. Shake hands with a half dozen players at your club. One will give you a "white knuckler" (a hard squeeze that turns your knuckles white); one will offer the "cold fish"; one the fingers closed "hammer grip"; one the "artist's grope" (fingers extended all over your palm and wrist); one a tip-of-the-fingers grab; and maybe one a normal firm but not death-grip shake with fingers slightly apart. But the variety is almost endless. And so are the kinds of grip.

My grips are anything but standard. I use the western grip for my forehand, which is rare among the pros. For the backhand I have the more accepted eastern, though my application is different from the norm; I drop my wrists so the racquet head is below the level of my hand. The racquet for my return of serve rests in the backhand grip, and for all other strokes, forehand volley, backhand volley, serve and overhead, I use the continental grip. (See photos.)

It's very important to hit the ball well in front of your hips. You can't see the ball properly if you let it get past your body. None of the pros hits the ball in back of him. Gerulaitis on his forehand is late occasionally, and Panatta sometimes, but he's so talented he can hit the ball with his hands over his eyes. Yet, on the volley don't hit as far in front as the books say. Hold your racquet 'way in front of you and see how flimsy it is. A ball hitting it in this position would receive no power. Now put your racquet just slightly in front, with your elbow pushed into your side, and feel the power and leverage.

Before 1976, whenever I came to net, I had the same grip as on my ground strokes, which meant that the forehand volley was hit with a western grip. It was impossible. That's why I had so many problems with my volley. If someone hit a dink to my forehand or backhand I usually dumped it into the net. When I changed to the continental grip I felt I had more time, and I could hit low balls effectively.

I made the change myself. I tried it more and more in practice. I saw just about everyone else use the continental and decided that if I was going to learn to volley I had better switch. No one had to tell me.

Other than this case of the volley, I never learned by imitation. I know others do, and watching the stars play is an

BJORN BORG

excellent way to learn, but I rarely notice the player; I follow the point instead. It never worried me that others were using different grips and strokes. I was stubborn.

Rod Laver was my childhood idol, but the first time I saw him in person was the 1971 Wimbledon, when he lost to Tom Gorman. Before that I watched him on TV, but his only influence on me was how he behaved on court, not his strokes. I admired his concentration and straight face. He never got upset. I wasn't too surprised on those rare occasions when he lost because he was playing with a Chemold metal racquet and I remember everyone in the locker room said the racquet was no damn good.

BACKHAND

There are many schools of thought about the advantages and disadvantages of the two-handed backhand. For example, some say that two hands share the work so it's less tiring; others say that because both hands are involved it's more tiring. I do know that I have to prepare earlier and bend my knees more on the two-handed shot than on my one-handed forehand. Other than that, I can only say that it works for me.

I place my right hand on the racquet as if the stroke were a standard one-handed eastern backhand. The left hand is placed above the right in a position in which I could hit a choked-up left-handed western forehand if I took my right hand away. I bring the racquet back slightly below my knees and close to my side with a small loop on the way back and both wrists cocked downward. I actually drop the racquet face below the level of my wrists to exaggerate the racquet head sweep from low to high, which also exaggerates the amount of top spin put on the return.

Jimmy Connors, on the other hand, brings his racquet straight back with a firm straight wrist slightly below his waist. Our different style results in a different type of shot. Connors' is flat, hard and deep, clearing the net by a few inches, but mine relies heavily on overspin, clearing the net by a foot or more and with varying depths.

As I pull the racquet forward, my wrists explode the rac-

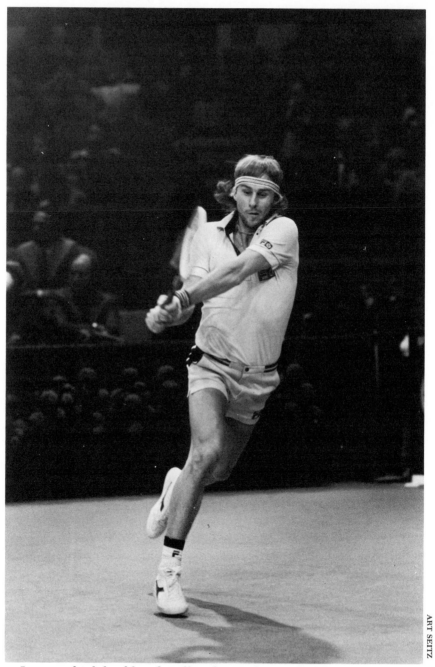

I meet a high backhand well in front of my right hip.

ART SEITZ

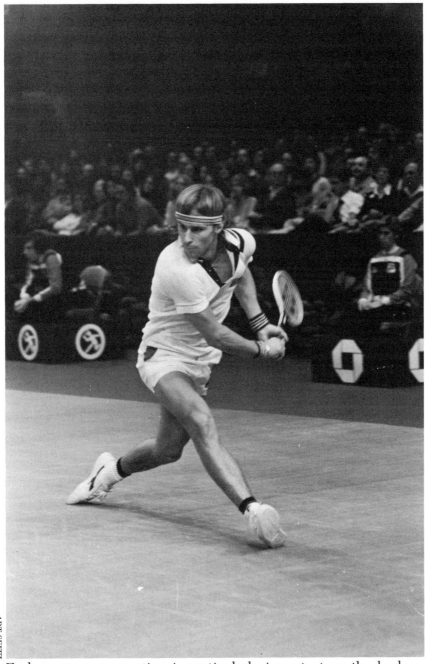

ART SEITZ

Early racquet preparation is particularly important on the back-hand.

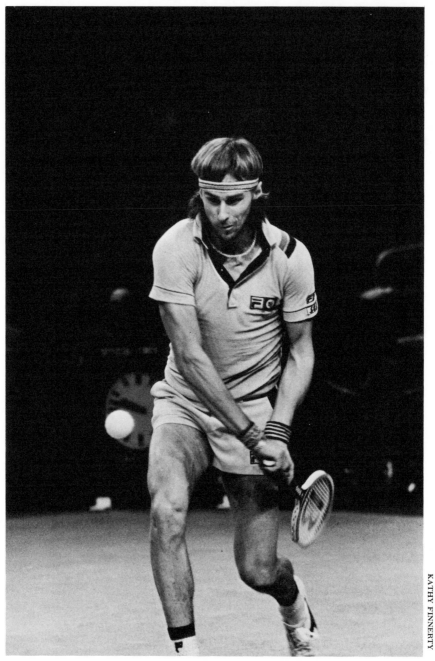

Here's the beginning of my forward swing on the backhand. Note that the racquet face is below the level of my wrists.

BJORN BORG

My backhand follow-through.

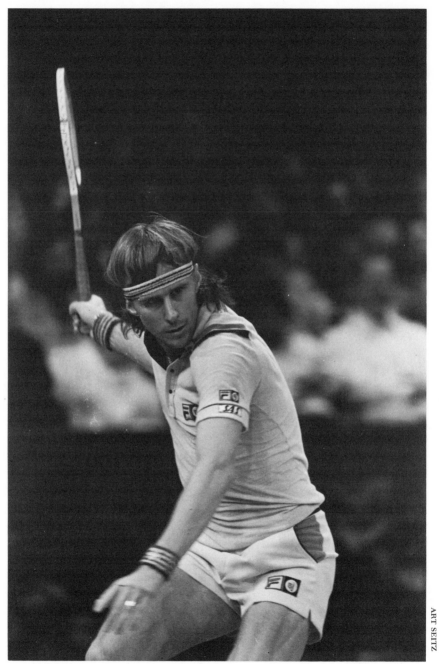

The middle of the loop on my forehand backswing.

Just before contact on a low bounce to my forehand. The racquet face is well below wrist level, and the shot requires keen concentration.

MY LIFE AND GAME

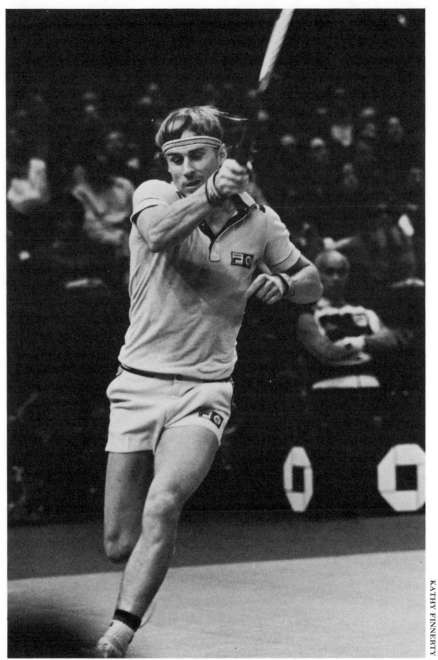

My forehand follow-through.

BJORN BORG

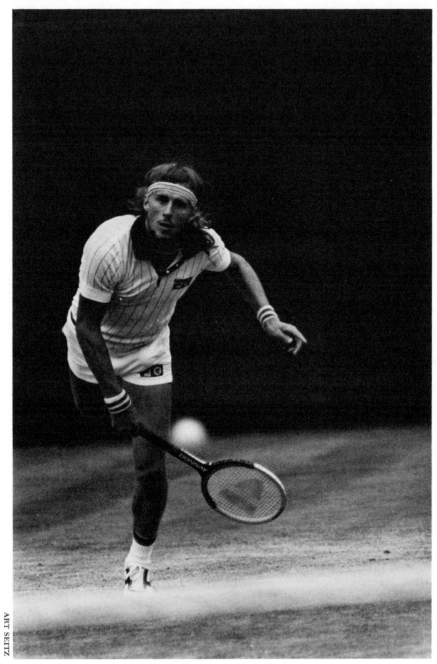

My follow-through on the serve.

MY LIFE AND GAME   137

quet face under the ball snapping upward to shoot tremendous top spin into the shot.

My right shoulder, which points toward the net on the backswing is parallel to the net at the end of the stroke, with the racquet head finishing on the right side of my body, two feet above my head on the follow-through. But the follow-through changes a lot on every stroke, depending on where the ball has bounced, where I want to hit it, and how much time I have.

My backhand is built for my game, patience in the backcourt and top-spin passing shots, while Connors' backhand is an offensive weapon, hit aggressively to draw a short return so Jimmy can attack at net. If I had to compare his backhand and mine in a few words, I'd say that mine is efficient, his is flamboyant.

FOREHAND

My grip on the forehand is western, with the heel of the racquet inside my palm, enabling my wrist to whip the racquet faster on its way to catch the ball. My stance is often open, which gives me more time to hit and get back into position. I do use my left hand to help take my racquet back. My backswing has a high loop, and I meet the ball well in front of my left hip (right hip in the open stance) striking between 4 and 5 o'clock if you imagine the ball as the face of a clock. I snap my wrists upward in a sweeping motion rolling the racquet face over at the end of contact and carrying the racquet over my left shoulder on the follow-through— often so it is pointing directly behind me.

Despite the speed of my arm and the racquet as it strikes the ball, my feet stay firmly on the ground and my hips move only slightly and do not roll forward the way a golfer's hips do. Keeping the lower body stable and low reduces power somewhat, but it is the key to my consistency.

The secret to my forehand is dropping the racquet head below the ball so the upward swing can produce wild top spin. Top spin can also be generated from the eastern grip but not as much. I do sacrifice depth by my heavy emphasis

Opposite, on my serve, as you can see, the grip is well within the palm of my right hand. Also, I'm standing sideways to the net almost until contact with the ball.   ART SEITZ on spin, but I think consistency is more important—not hitting over the base line nor hitting into the net.

THE SERVE

I don't serve as hard as Tanner, Nastase, DuPre, Fleming or McEnroe, but my first serve is effective because it is difficult to pick. My motion is simple, with no fancy wind-up, and I hit it down the line or at an angle from the same toss, making its direction difficult to anticipate. My second serve has pretty heavy spin, and while it's not an offensive weapon, no one can attack it easily.

I keep the second ball in my left pocket, not in my hand, because I need my left hand for the two-fisted backhand, but I also think it's a good idea for anyone. Fetching the ball from the pocket makes you slow down instead of rushing the second serve right after the first fault. In addition, a free left hand is a better guide to help take the racquet back on both forehand and backhand.

My service motion is very simple, though I have had problems with my toss in the past. You want to make sure the toss goes straight up and does not move in an arc. I face the side of the court when I start to serve and if my toss is straight in front of me the ball has a tendency to sail slightly backward over my head in a curve. To offset this problem, I toss the ball in front of my left side toward the net.

In 1976, when Lennart and I decided I had to improve my serve, the first thing we did was change my foot position at the start of the serve. My right, or trailing, foot is now directly behind my front foot, which forms the top of the letter T. With my trailing foot this far behind, I feel that more of my body gets into the serve and not just my arm as before. John McEnroe exaggerates this trailing-foot position even more with his back foot almost touching the base line. My follow through is conventional, with the racquet ending up past my left side.

Tennis doesn't often reward the dazzling shot, especially on a slow surface. For instance, if you hit a marvelous flat serve deep into the backhand corner on clay, it is a mindless

140

tactic. The speed and depth are blunted by the court, and the risk, energy and concentration required to deliver a well-placed megablast serve is simply not worth it.

I do put an enormous amount of spin on both first and second serves for consistency—the second is not aimed even close to the lines. I just put this one deep in the middle of the service box with enough spin so my opponent can't chip and charge the net. I never try to win the point outright on my serve, nor should you. In the finals of the French Championships in 1979 I didn't serve a single ace. The most I do is change direction and amount of spin for surprise. I may make Connors miss my serve because he is caught off guard, but not because I ace him.

On a fast surface—grass, cement, a slick indoor court—it is smart for a good server to go for the ace. The percentages are now better because, if the ball goes in hard, the surface won't slow it down. In other words, you get a reward for a lightning serve at Wimbledon, while at the French it usually doesn't help at all.

The problem about beginners and intermediates going for a bullet first serve is that if they miss they're faced with having to get the second one in. This is the most embarrassing situation for any player—the humiliation of hitting a double fault. Avoid it by concentrating totally on hitting the second serve. Don't bother practicing the first. Anyone can hit the ball hard, but only a handful in the world can put the hard ones in with any consistency. The old theory that "you are only as good as your second serve" is one of the few lessons from the past that are still true—even for the superstars. After I broke Tanner's serve in the first game of the fifth set in the '79 Wimbledon Finals, I hit nothing but good second serves as my first the rest of the day. In other words, I played it safe, because I didn't want Tanner to see a first serve miss and gain confidence knowing a second serve was coming. That way he'd be attacking the net on my service games.

Roscoe obviously is from another school. He banged over two dozen unplayable serves against me in five sets. But I won the match.

Perhaps the best example for 98 percent of the world's

players to follow is the playing of Chris Evert Lloyd and Tracy Austin in the 1979 U.S. Open final, on a fast, asphalt surface, where neither hit an ace in the match. Still they played each other beautifully and wisely. The ace is a dramatic shot—like the home run in baseball—but it may destroy your sense of tactics by tempting you to hit the ball harder than is safe. A simple home run can win a baseball game but a single ace can't win a tennis match.

One of the temptations intermediate players have is to follow their serves to net just like the "big boys." Even at my level of the game I think this is wrong. But at lower levels I think the strategy invariably is suicide. Sure, it may work sometimes, but you'll probably remember your one brilliant cross-court volley and forget about the two flubs and the passing shot hit by you. The volley is the toughest shot to master, and if you serve and just hit a safe volley, it is a set-up for your foe's forehand. In other words, his ground strokes are better than your volley, and unless you prepare your way carefully to volley by rallying until you get a short ball, and then underspinning a deep approach, you'll just find yourself at net begging to be passed.

VOLLEY

One of the main reasons the volley is the most difficult stroke to perfect is that no one practices the volley one tenth as much as any other stroke. Most of us when we start to rally, hit for ten minutes in the back court, come to net for five volleys, two overheads, and then say, "I'm ready, let's play."

The problem about properly learning the volley is that it can't be practiced politely. What we all do is go to net and hit the volley right back to our practice partner so he won't get mad at our "rude" put-aways. The bad habit starts here. The volley is supposed to be an offensive weapon. There should be no such thing as a steady volleyer. You're not at the net to rally. But when you practice one up, one back, you never get a sense of putting the volley away. The only way this can be learned is by using a ball machine, whose feelings can't be hurt when you go for volley winners—or by getting a third practice mate and rotating the one person at net with two in the back court so that everyone gets a chance at hitting the volley aggressively. With two players at the base line, the balls that would have been "rude" put-aways with one person will be returned. If a third player isn't available, at least station the base-line person in the backhand or forehand side of the court to give a semblance of reality to the practice session. Few players hit their volley down the middle and live to talk about it.

The best teaching line about volleying I credit to Pancho Gonzalez, who said that when he was at net he hit the ball pretending the barrier was not there. "I don't volley over the net," Pancho says. "I volley into the court." Pancho's advice may be the first Zen tennis advice. It makes sense. How many of us worry about getting the ball over the net when we should be aiming for a space in the back court?

On the backhand volley, I get my racquet 'way back shoulder high past my left ear, with the racquet pointing behind my body. I only have half as big a wind-up on my forehand volley. When you don't have much time you can only block or punch at the volley, but if you have hit a good approach shot, you should be prepared to take a solid crack at the ball. The volley is supposed to be an offensive stroke, and if you're not prepared to put the ball away, you shouldn't be at net. How often do you see a net man hit a defensive safe volley and get passed the next shot? I come to net as often in a match as I do in practice—which on a slow surface (clay, Har-Tru, Fast-Dri) is 5 percent of the time. On a faster surface the percentage may increase to 10 percent, but no more.

I don't bend my knees as low as Connors does. His bending must take a lot of energy out of him. Connors bends so much and gets so low to the ball that his right knee sometimes touches the court surface. A statistical expert once estimated that in a normal two-set match on clay lasting one hour, there are approximately 2,500 ball hits, not including faults. If I bent my knees as low as Connors, I'd be exhausted considering 1,250 of those ball hits were mine. Part-time players aren't in the same shape that Connors is and I'd advise them not to copy him. You just don't have to bend your knees that much to play properly. We both meet the ball well in front of our hips and, like all two-handers, must prepare the stroke extra early.

If one looks for the origins of Bjorn's game that combine the apparent contradiction of thunderous top spin and metronome steadiness, we find that it is no contradiction at all. The top spin is, after all, the means to his consistency. If his style looks like Ping-pong without rushing the net, it is no accident. His father, Rune, narrowly missed being named to the Swedish table-tennis team twice, and the influence of Ping-pong is everywhere in Borg's strokes. One of Bjorn's childhood games was makeshift Ping-pong, with books being used as a net on the dining room table.

Tennis demanded that he learn a counterattack dimension that Ping-pong did not require—the passing shot. Borg could have chosen the flashy flat pass or the conservative slice of many of his Swedish forebears, Jan Erik Lundquist, Sven Davidson, or his own coach Lennart Bergelin. Characteristically, he selected instead a method that was safer than no-spin and more effective than underspin. Excessive top spin would clear the net by a foot or more yet dip at the attacker's feet. It has force, deception, and consistency. It also is in the immediate family of his ground strokes. He does not have to adjust his motion from ground stroke to passing shot. Many players have an arsenal of shots so varied that the sheer weight of choice is confusing and obstructs what should be the easy flow of the game.

BEGINNERS AND TOP SPIN

Obviously a beginner has trouble enough making contact with the ball so my top-spin trademark is not appropriate until you have a proper sense of timing and reasonably strong wrists.

A beginner, on the other hand, has to concentrate on the basics, which include taking the racquet straight back with no loops or fancy hitches and rotating the shoulders simultaneously. The wrist should be slightly cocked, with the racquet head just above the level of the wrists. The arc of the swing should be from a little below the hip to head high. The beginner should keep a firm wrist throughout the forehand and backhand strokes. Ideally, the left foot should be parallel to the net and two feet in front of the right foot on the forehand, and on the backhand the right foot should similarly be parallel to the net and two feet in front of the left foot. But tennis is not played under ideal conditions. You never get a ball dropped carefully a foot in front of your body so you can slowly deliberate on your stroke. You are hitting a moving ball while you too are moving. A beginner rarely is successful at staying low to the ball and following through. More often he retreats awkwardly and makes his hit with left or right leg raised off the ground. He is perilously close to falling down. A sense of balance and timing cannot be taught by book. It must be learned on court by constantly experiencing the speed and spin of balls traveling in any direction.

There are two basic schools of thought on how to develop terrific top spin. One is to start swinging the racquet slowly with slight overspin and, once your confidence and timing are developed, to pick up the velocity of the stroke gradually until the wrist snap and swing are going full bore. The other technique is to start right away at full blast, which surely means hitting a lot of balls into the net and over the fence, but the theory is that once you've mastered the speed, there is no further adjustment required. I feel that that is right. The graduated method is not efficient, because as you learn each level it must be unlearned when you pick up the pace.

My advice, so you don't lose practice partners as often as you lose balls in the parking lot, is to practice your top spin with a ball machine, hitting hundreds of balls full out until you get the feel of the wrist snap and catching the ball just right. Your first target should just be the center of the court, and, as you develop your timing, you alter your aim gradually, from side to side.

I know that two of the past greats, Don Budge and Jack Kramer have kidded about my top-spin shots, which sometimes land shallow near the service line. One of Budge's favorite quips is that he hit his serve with greater depth than my ground strokes. To respond to this would get me into the same sort of never-ending argument as to who was better,

Bill Tilden or Rod Laver? I guess I don't care what the old-timers think. The last Hall of Famer I listened to told me I could never win Wimbledon with a western forehand, a two-handed backhand and not coming to net. I'm willing to let my record speak for itself.

CHAPTER

8

Getting Your Mind

Over the Net

"Borg has tunnel vision. He pays the price. He can stay on court literally all day hitting forehands and backhands. He wants to be out there in 100°, in the humidity, under a boiling sun."

—BILLIE JEAN KING

Do you remember that racquet design didn't change for almost a hundred years? The construction was wood and egg-shaped—not different for a century. It makes you wonder what sort of people made racquets—were they made of wood and egg-shaped too?

Tennis instruction has suffered from the same lack of imagination for almost as long. Players have been fed an identical patter for years, as if all abilities were equal and as if what made sense for one athlete made sense for everyone, with no sense of the individual built into the lesson.

Variety should be not only permitted but required in learning the full range of any stroke—and also for adjustments as the learning process goes on. For instance, if you put too much wrist into any shot, one correction is to move the hand further up the handle so the butt end comes out of the palm to prevent a floppy wrist. My standard grip on both forehand and backhand has the butt end of the racquet flush against the fleshy part of my right palm, which means that my hand overlaps the end of the racquet. This makes my wrist flexible so that it can snap violently at the ball giving enormous top spin. However, if I suggested the same grip to a student trying to learn flat, deep ground strokes, it would be disastrous. For precision and accuracy on forehands and backhands with no spin, a firm wrist is essential. Grasping the handle so that the heel sticks slightly out of the hand is one way to achieve a stiff wrist.

SPIN

Grips and spin are closely related, and both involve choices that you must make in deciding what sort of game you want to play. The more spin you put on the ball the more power you lose. Jimmy Connors hits the ball harder than I do, but his passing shots sometimes are not as effective as mine because they have little deception and no margin for error. When Jimmy is on, he is devastating, because even if you know where he is going to hit the ball, he hits it so hard that anticipation doesn't help. But day in and day out, my results may be better because my passes are more consistent; and it is difficult to volley my ball dipping at your feet. Connors' drives rise as they go over the net and a good volleyer prefers this to hitting below the net.

There is one concept that you should understand before you decide which style you prefer—top spin with reduced power but good safety, or flat with more power but less safety. My top spin is safe, but not because it is accurate in depth. On a passing shot I don't care whether the ball lands close to the base line or the service line. If the ball passes the man at net, it doesn't count more if it lands on the base line. But I do need a ball that goes straight and is not affected by the wind. Top spin, no matter how wristy, can go straight as a string down the line or cross-court and will not be blown off line by a gust of wind as easily as will a flat or sliced ball.

The second reason why top spin is safe is that it clears the net by a larger margin than a a flat or sliced shot. It is not

BJORN BORG

important whether the ball clears the net by six inches or by two feet on sinking shots.

To your opponent the difference between your clearing the net by six inches and clearing it by two feet is his having to hit the volley off his shoe tops or below his knees—both are difficult. A hard, flat ground stroke, on the other hand, has to skim the net closely to be effective and thus increases the chances that the ball will hit the net. And a slice, while it can clear the net by a wide margin in base-line rallies, is useless as a passing shot unless one has the genius for precision that Ken Rosewall had.

The one drawback of top spin for beginners and intermediate players is that you must have remarkable timing to avoid hitting the ball off the frame. If you're having difficulty making proper contact with the ball, go back to hitting flat, keeping the stroke as simple as possible. Remember, the style you decide on should be dictated by your own ability —not by a desire to copy Connors or me.

For me, top spin is preferable for many reasons. Not only does it give fits to net rushers, but it allows for my steadiness

Part of "getting your mind over the net" is the feeling that you are a champion.

E. L. SCOTT

in the back court. I can clear the net with enormous safety, and even if the ball lands short at the service line, the spin will carry the ball past the base line. So I have the best of both worlds—safety plus depth. Naturally, against a good player, I hit at an opponent's service line at my peril. He is very likely to pounce on the ball and come to net. But he had better hit a perfect approach or my top-spin pass will be at his feet. I try to keep my ground strokes at least between the service line and the base line and let the top spin provide the rest of the stroke's depth, but I do have the safety valve of knowing that even though a slight mishit can change the depth by two or three feet, the ball will still land in court. A hard flat hitter like Connors doesn't have that luxury, since he is aiming for the vicinity of the base line every time. If he hits slightly off center, a two- or three-foot variation will lose him the point.

There are two other reasons why I prefer the top-spin approach. One is that not only is the dipping action treacherous for a volleyer, but the shot is very flexible. You can change its direction at the last minute by flipping the wrist, making the shot impossible to read. And finally the top-spin arc of the ball gives you more time to recover from an off-court position. The result is that top spin combines a safe yet deceptive offensive weapon with defensive features built in.

Kids eight years old don't respond to the words, "take your racquet back," "watch the ball," and "bend your knees" as well as they do to their own instincts of how to hit the ball. Saying, "watch the ball" is insulting to a child. Of course, he's trying to watch the ball. Saying too much is distracting. "Take the racquet back" is another standard phrase. It's silly. Of course he'll take the racquet back without being told. What is useful is to urge the youngster to take his racquet back *early*, because that advice helps right away. He'll have more time to prepare the stroke. You can even elaborate on this point by telling him to take his racquet back when the ball passes over the net. This gives a target to think about.

Saying "bend your knees" is meaningless. No youngster with any athletic ability will hit even his first shot stiff-legged. He'll do what's comfortable. John McEnroe and Peter Fleming stand almost straight up when they hit the ball, while Jimmy Connors goes almost to his knees on every forehand and backhand. But that takes a lot of energy. Generally I'd recommend having a stance that is a compromise between proper balance and comfort.

A golfer addresses the ball with his hips at right angles to the direction of the shot, and, at the moment of impact, his hips rotate rapidly so on follow-through they face straight down the fairway. There is little such hip rotation in tennis. My hips remain perfectly still at impact, and even on follow-through they rarely move in the direction of the ball. Also I never lift off my feet on follow-through, no matter how hard I swing at the ball. Many players jump off the ground when they hit top spin, on the theory that the violent upward motion of the stroke takes them off their feet. I maintain that for both power and accuracy the momentum of the swing should be not *up*, but forward. There is very little movement in my lower body in the swing zone. My wrist, arm and shoulder provide all the power I need. If the rest of my body gets involved, there is too much unnecessary motion, which destroys the stroke's precision.

In choosing basic styles—ground stroker or volleyer or a combination of both—you should be aware that even for a weekend player, staying in the back court will take more out of you than volleying. You will have to be in better shape to rally all day than ending points quickly by moving to net. With each opponent you must weigh the factors—am I in better condition? am I steadier? do I have a better volley?

Try to make the choice simple. Reduce the game to its simplest terms, so you don't have to worry about execution of shots you don't have. Most players learn how to hit ground strokes first. The volley is the game's most difficult stroke to learn not only because its mechanics are intricate, but because the time spent learning the volley is so proportionately small, as I've explained earlier.

What is anticipation? It is moving to a part of the court before your opponent hits the ball. Part of this is simply experience, knowing the smart shot for the other man to hit in every situation. For example, if you both are in the back court and you hit a backhand deep to your opponent's backhand, the safest shot for him is to return to your backhand. So you'd

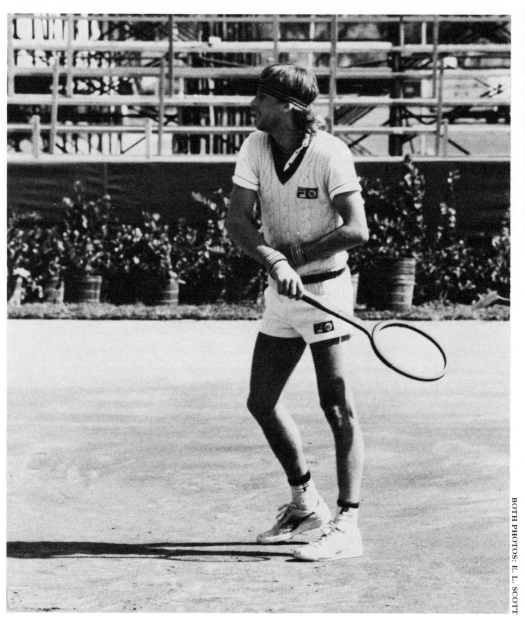

The problem with standardized instruction is that it confuses students who see the pros do things differently from the way instructors advise. The fact is that I almost never hit the ball exactly the same way twice. My backhand and forehand follow-throughs, shown above and opposite, are not typical even for me, but all worked on these particular shots.

BJORN BORG

move instinctively in this direction. Yet if you came to net behind the same deep approach to the backhand, you'd lean to the forehand forecourt, because the court angle makes it impossible to play the same safe cross-court shot without you cutting it off at the net.

What are the most important points in a match? For once, convention is correct on the subject—15–30, 30–15, break point, and the first point of every game. But I've never hesitated beforehand to consider how I was going to win these points. I have played so many practice matches and so many tournaments that my game is instinctive. It happens that when I'm even or ahead and have a long point to play—break point, set point or ad against me—my instinct is always to play safe. If I'm behind, I take a chance and go for it. If I'm going to lose, I don't care—I'll hit away.

I don't have four different ways to play—I just own one game—top spin and patience from the back court. Because the plan is simple, it is easier to concentrate, there are no distractions, no problems.

I don't have to rely on a particular strategy other than keeping the ball deep and high over the net to cut down on errors; nor do I use any rally sequence if an opponent has a weakness. My selecting shots to probe his weaknesses is at random. In this way I can play by instinct and not get bogged down by having to think where I'm going to place the ball each time.

The process of deliberating how and where to hit the ball is incredibly tiring, and because I have the ability to turn on the "automatic pilot" and not fret over each shot, spectators think I'm so "cool under pressure." Doctors say my low pulse rate is healthy too; it means that my heart can send blood through my system with less pumping than my opponent's heart may have to do to accomplish the same function.

TRAINING

One of the worst abuses by tennis players is what they drink at courtside. Usually it is whatever product—Coke, Iced Tea,

Tab, Pepsi, etc.—is supplied free to the tournament director in exchange for the beverage company's exposure on court. Many times these companies pay enormous fees to have exclusive identification at courtside; Coke pays the U.S. Open $250,000 per year to have their giant Coke sign above the scoreboard and coolers by the umpire's chair. Other smaller events receive $2,500 to $25,000 each, depending on television coverage. When a company pays this sort of money, they insist on having their product on hand in their cooler and served in their cups. The tournament director does nothing to upset this routine although a player is perfectly within his rights to bring his own concoction on court. Some do. But 90 percent of the touring pros simply drink the sponsor's goo in the cooler.

Jimmy Connors, for example, drinks Coke throughout his match. I drink only water. During a three-hour *practice* session, I will drink three quarts of cold water, but only one quart during a three-hour match. Neither Lennart nor I subscribe to the theory that cold liquids give you stomach cramps. We feel that if you're hot, cold water cools you off, warm water does not. In any case, I've been drinking ice water for the sixteen years of my tennis career and never have had stomach cramps.

My training for a tournament is done beforehand. Once a tournament begins, I rarely practice for more than an hour unless I have a day off. My warm-up before a final is even less—twenty minutes to a half hour, just like a guitarist who picks and tunes before a concert. This really isn't for practice at all, but for timing. If I had a vigorous session right before an important match, it would take the edge off. If I'm not in shape by Sunday, I won't get there by hitting for two hours that morning.

I never run for conditioning before or during any championship. The only time I ever jog is when I'm at home for a rest. I gain weight unbelievably without tennis—then I go out for a run to keep my weight around 160.

I think for others it is a good idea to run—not long distances like the marathoners or even the joggers, but short-step running. Quick sprints are helpful. You don't run a mile in a tennis match, you run a thousand ten-foot races. I do all my running on court by practicing four, five and six hours a day.

I don't stay away from any foods in particular. I eat bread, butter, milk and especially ice cream, all of which are traditionally too fatty for an athlete's diet, but I don't care what I eat when I'm playing. I burn up all the foods I eat, so I never gain weight. Obviously, if you play only on weekends it's hard to get your system rid of the junk foods. If you have a giant steak and potatoes the same night I do, and the next day I play five sets and you don't, you'll wear your meal around your middle for a month. And every extra pound you carry around is a huge handicap. Just imagine putting a five-pound weight in your shorts and trying to play tennis.

When I stop playing I do watch what I eat, avoiding sweets and often taking only one meal a day. I don't like hard liquor and drink only wine and beer. I've never smoked.

I know my diet of meat and vegetables is old-fashioned for athletes. The accepted training meal today is a menu loaded with carbohydrates like bread, potatoes and all forms of pasta. Tennis players first heard of this when Adriano Panatta was seen preparing for the French and Italian Open on large helpings of spaghetti. The players ridiculed him at first, saying this was another example of the talented Italian's lack of discipline. Then he won the Italian and French Open back to back in 1976 and people listened.

THE LOB

One more myth is how difficult the top-spin lob is. Nonsense. The reason it seems so impossible is that no one practices it. Have you ever seen a player with a basket of balls go onto a court and practice his top-spin lob? Of course not. The same is true of the drop shot. No one works on craft and disguise in practice (at least you try the drop shot in enough matches over the years to develop a feel for the stroke). But because it is considered rude to your partner to practice something he can't work on at the same time, both the top-spin lob and the drop shot are neglected. The answer, if course, is talking about the problem beforehand with your practice partner and taking turns developing these never-drilled strokes. The top-spin lob, because of its deception, adds incredible dimensions to your game and is possibly easier to hit than a good deep, flat lob. (Anyone can hit a ball up in the air and call it a lob, but the accuracy and timing required to loft a ball without spin on the run and have it land close to the base line is extremely delicate.)

Actually, the top-spin lob doesn't have to be as deep as the flat one, because it's so difficult to read.

I do not lob well defensively; because I have so much confidence in my passing shots, I don't practice the defensive lob. I like the offensive lob, which is a sudden high top-spinner that I hit with the same stance as a passing shot—so the netman is leaning forward when the ball sails over his head.

PERCENTAGE TENNIS

My conservative game forces rivals to take chances. If they do, the percentages work for me. If an opponent like Roscoe Tanner serves twenty-five aces against me in a match, he'll probably win, but he can't do this very often. My game forces him to play low-percentage tennis.

Percentage tennis means different things to different players. Jack Kramer's percentage tennis represents the traditional thinking that used to make sense. "Never serve to your opponent's forehand on a big point," and "Always underspin your approach (so it stays low forcing him to hit up) to your opponent's backhand"—these were Kramer mainstays. And for his era they worked. In the old days, no one except Don Budge had a backhand weapon, one that was more dangerous than the forehand. Today, there are a dozen players, including Arthur Ashe, Jimmy Connors, Cliff Drysdale, John McEnroe and myself, who like nothing better than an opponent who hits to our backhand on a big point.

My definition of percentage tennis is different. It's not so much a matter of whether I hit to my opponent's forehand or to his backhand, because I think I can run down any attack and counterpunch effectively, no matter where the ball is hit. My synonym for percentage tennis is *patience*. I want to hit one more ball in court than my rival. I want him to think I'm much more patient so he'll make a mistake either in execution (racquet error) or in picking a low-percentage ripper for the lines. This philosophy works for beginners too. If a novice (or an intermediate player, for that matter) plays my way, he will aim most of his shots cross-court, where there is more room for mistakes. If you aim a ball down the line and miss by an inch, you'll lose the point. But if you always think cross-court you can miss by two yards or more and still have the ball land safely in court.

Even I practice these beginner patterns when I'm having difficulty adjusting to strange conditions or to a particular opponent. I keep the ball in the center of the court, waiting until I have grooved my strokes.

Kramer was the first proponent of the Big Game, in which he followed both his first serve and his second serve to net on any fast surface and rushed in to volley even on his opponent's serve. Jack's percentages were set forth in terms of all-out attack. Frankly, this appears to be a contradiction to me. I'm not saying he wasn't successful. He was. And he certainly was a great player. But he didn't play percentage tennis the way I think of it—in terms of safety and caution. A net rusher is not playing it safe. He is daring you to pass him. Kramer won because he was bold and had the skills to back it up. He didn't play percentage tennis.

My "percentages" have more to do with my mind than with my strokes. I try to make my challenger believe he can't outsteady me. My cold attitude on court helps. I never applaud or acknowledge an opponent's good shot. I just go about my business, the next point. This, in a sense, is saying, "I don't care how spectacular one shot is, you'll have to hit two thousand exactly like it to beat me."

Remember that at the top levels of the game, weaknesses and strengths are only relative. In a sense, there are no weaknesses only comparative strengths. But this is not entirely true. There are fifty players who can volley better than I or Vilas. But we both have found that if our ground strokes are good enough, we literally don't need a volley to win. We can't be as reluctant to come up to net as Harold Solomon, but we both understand that we volley for surprise and to add a sudden dimension to our games when our opponents least expect it.

There is a standard littany offered by instructors when Borg's name is brought up. "No one else can play the way he does," or "I'd never try to teach Bjorn Borg's strokes." Because the Swede's strokes are unorthodox and he was, to a large extent, self-taught, tennis teachers cringe at the prospect of their students imitating Borg's style. That is a commentary about the reactionary mentality of teaching pros more than anything else. The fact that Borg has won four French Opens (considered by experts as the world's clay-court championships and the game's most grueling test) and four Wimbledons in a row on grass should mean that he must be doing something right, and that there is something for the rest of tennis mankind to learn from him.

CARICATURE BY DAVID LEVINE

CHAPTER

9

Album

In picking my ten best matches, the criteria for selection include the significance of when and where the match was played. For instance, I didn't include the 1978 final of the $200,000 Suntory Cup in Tokyo, where I destroyed Connors and lost only four games in the process. The event was only a four-man round robin with enormous guarantees paid to all of us regardless of who won. It didn't have any sense of tradition and history and had no rank as an important title on the calendar. In fact, because the field was limited to four, the results counted neither for world ranking nor for official prize money. But the tennis was terrific. Jimmy too played well, but on that day I was lucky and won every important point.

Also I don't include any losses, even though I may have played well. If I had to list a few defeats I remember well, surely my four-setter to John Newcombe in the 1975 WCT finals and the five-set marathon to Roger Taylor in the 1973 Wimbledon quarters, come to mind. But no match I have lost helped me to reach my goal of winning more major titles than any tennis player in history.

I have chosen a single match from the list to record the multiple elements of competition with reflections that are something between a sketchbook and a diary.

BORG'S 10 BIGGEST WINS

1. Davis Cup 1972   Borg over Onny Parun
   4–6, 3–6, 6–3, 6–4, 6–4

2. French Open Finals 1974   Borg over Manuel Orantes
   2–6, 6–7, 6–0, 6–1, 6–1

3. WCT Semi-final 1975   Borg over Rod Laver
   7–6, 3–6, 7–6, 6–2

4. Wimbledon Final 1976   Borg over Ilie Nastase
   6–4, 6–2, 9–7

5. Wimbledon Semi-final 1977   Borg over Vitas Gerulaitis
   6–4, 3–6, 6–3, 3–6, 8–6

6. Wimbledon Final 1977   Borg over Jimmy Connors
   3–6, 6–2, 6–1, 5–7, 6–4

7. Barcelona Grand Prix 1977   Borg over Eddie Dibbs
   6–0, 6–0, 6–2

8. Wimbledon Final 1978   Borg over Jimmy Connors
   6–2, 6–2, 6–3

9. Wimbledon Semi-final 1979   Borg over Jimmy Connors
   6–2, 6–3, 6–2

10. Masters Round Robin 1980   Borg over Jimmy Connors
    3–6, 6–3, 7–6

THE MATCH

Jimmy Connors has been my most intense rival for six years. John McEnroe has the game right now to give both Jimmy and me fits—his style is flexible, while Jimmy's is rigid. John can open up the entire court with his serve, and his volley is lightning, but the fury of a McEnroe-Borg rivalry has not yet had a chance to boil over. It's still simmering.

Connors and I, on the other hand, have been at each other's throats for five U.S. Opens and four Wimbledons. I have the edge now 14 to 10 in total matches, but in the early going, Jimmy totally intimidated me even on my favorite surface, clay.

Nineteen seventy-nine was my best year for dominating

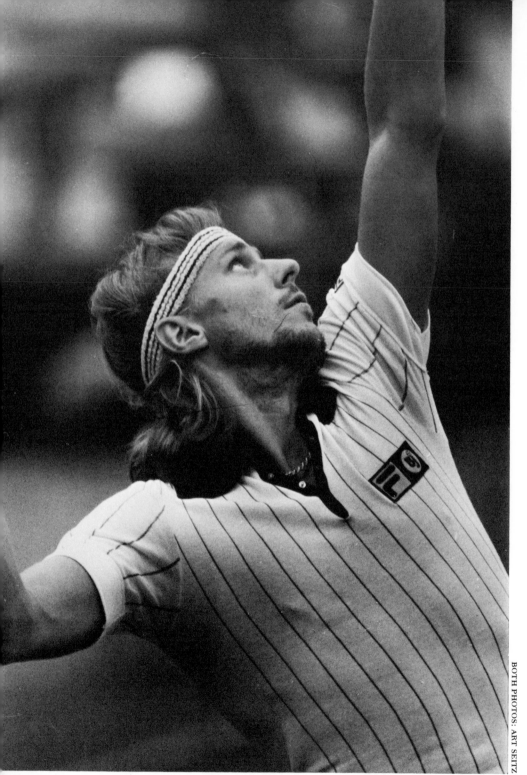

At Wimbledon in the course of my victories there.

More action at Wimbledon.

Connors when I won six times and never lost—plus another match at the Grand Prix Masters in 1980, which is really considered part of the 1979 season. The latter was the most exciting encounter I have ever experienced against Jimmy— maybe anybody. Other titles have been more prestigious or worth more prize money, or both, but none has matched the fire of that Thursday night of January 10 at Madison Square Garden.

To set the stage, Connors was coming off a mediocre year for him—he reached the semis of the French, Wimbledon, and the U.S. Open, won the U.S. Clay Courts and six other tournaments and $701,340 in prize money. Mediocre for Jimmy meant that for the first time in five years he was ranked number two on the computer. He had reasons for his apparent letdown. He had married former playmate of the year Patti Maguire at the end of 1978. They had a baby boy, Brett, in July 1979, and the experience distracted Jimmy from his tennis. I could see that. He plays with such intensity and his margin for error is so low, that any lapse in concentration is fatal to his game.

He kept saying that once his marriage and son were in order, he would be back. The first sign of this spirit was at the $300,000 Montreal Challenge Cup in December 1979. We both reached the finals and, although I won in four sets, the second set—which he won—was the best he had played against me in two years.

The Masters came exactly a month later, and Jimmy was especially lean—he had lost almost ten pounds—and you could see electricity in his eyes. He seemed to be in a barely controlled rage all week, and it was obvious in his play.

The shame was that the round-robin pairings had Jimmy and me in the same group. After all, we were ranked first and second in the world and should have been split up. However, the policy of the Masters is to seed players according to their standings in the Grand Prix, which rewards the number of events played—good to encourage participation in tournaments around the world—but poor as a method for picking seeds. As a result I would have to beat Roscoe Tanner, who had upset me at the U.S. Open four months earlier, and Connors to reach the semi-finals.

Before I went on court that night, Bill Norris, one of the official tour trainers limbered up my legs for ten minutes with a cream from a large white bottle of Dermassage body lotion. Norris has dubbed himself "The Wizard of Gauze," a label that he has had printed on the back of his Adidas track suit, which he parades on court at every opportunity.

The match starts at 8:00 P.M. Although I break Connors right away to lead 2–0 in the first set, there are sparks shooting out of his socks. Jimmy breaks back immediately, and with a series of deep hard base-line exchanges, he dictates the pace of each game. This is a dedicated confident Connors I hadn't seen in a long time. By 9:05, Jimmy had won the first set, 6–3.

I'm playing terrible. I'm just out of the match. If I continue to play like this I don't deserve to win. Connors is on top of every ball and hits it really well.

Connors plays a loose service game to open the second set, and I break straightway. Maybe I can get into the match. I've just got to be more aggressive. I must take some chances, attack his serve.

Lennart sitting in the third row of Madison Square Garden's courtside seats has not said a word. His arms are folded, and they would remain so through the entire match, except that every so often he slowly unfolds his arms and drys his palms on the thighs of his gray-flannel trousers. The only sound from Lennart is a dry crackling noise when his mouth opens, which is the dead giveaway of his nervousness.

My fiancée, Mariana, sits next to him, and they will not exchange a single sentence the entire match. She alternately sighs and bites her lip. And whispers, "Jesus Christ," under her breath after every important point. It is fitting that the two people closest to me behave on the sidelines as I do on court—quiet and intent.

Finally Lennart speaks—to no one in particular; eyes straight ahead—"Bjorn must actually win a game, not just let Connors lose it, before he'll believe he can win."

Nine-thirty. I miss another forehand, and if you looked closely, you would have seen my first sign of emotion—a slight shake of my head. Nine-forty. I uncork a bolo forehand for a quick winner from the back court. Nine-forty-five. As I sit down on the changeover, I notice Andy Warhol sitting in the front row with his arms folded exactly like Lennart. Nine-forty-seven. Crowd applauds a Connors fault, and I'm puzzled—if the fans behave like animals how can anyone wonder why the players don't control themselves?

There is a unique anticlapping custom among professionals. If you look at the players' section in any stadium, you will find that the pros don't applaud good shots. The reason? Showing favoritism would haunt a player who one day would face the man he cheered against.

It's a simple extension of the Golden Rule. No player wants to be antagonized by his fellow players and so he won't do it himself. Nine-fifty. I flub an easy backhand volley to give Connors 40–15, his serve, second set, but I'm ahead 4–2. After an exhausting rally I burn a forehand down the line. Then a backhand. Deuce. Connors has lost his glow. He misses a forehand approach and I outsteady him from the base line. My game—I lead, 5–2. Nine-fifty-seven. I double-fault twice to lose serve letting Connors close to 3–5.

The price of Connors' intensity is fatigue. Not the type where he is huffing and puffing. More subtle. The brain is just not sending messages to his forehand as efficiently as it was doing earlier. The result is obvious. Ten-seven. I break Jimmy for the third time in the set to square the match 3–6, 6–3.

Ten-twelve. Connors' service grunt becomes a loud hack —30 all, 0–1, final set. He's missing his first serve frequently now. Break point. I thunder a forehand down the line but miss by an inch. Deuce. Frank Hammond, the well known Chair Umpire, calls the score wrong giving me the game. He makes the correction quickly adding, "I'm sorry, I'm sorry, I'm sorry," in a descending scale so that his last apology is barely audible. A year ago the proud Hammond would never have apologized from the chair, but last September at the U. S. Open he was involved in a wild melee with Ilie Nastase and John McEnroe on the Stadium Court. He was so embarrassed at being removed as umpire that he nearly quit officiating for good. The memory lingers. Hammond may be apologizing for the match four months ago.

Ten-fifteen. Lennart smacks his lips that dry crackling

sound. Ten-seventeen. Connors asks me for confirmation that his forehand was out as called. I nod and smile. He smiles back. Despite a $100,000 purse to the winner and the enormous pride each of us has in not wanting to lose to his fiercest rival, there is still respect. Ten–twenty-one. I hold to 2–1 final set. Mariana crosses her legs nervously and bites her lip at the same time. Lennart smacks again. Connors plays a loose game, and I break to 3–1.

I think to myself this must be the best early-round match in the game's history. In every other tournament that goes according to form, the number one and two meet in the finals. But in the weird world of round-robins, we could play again in the finals if both of us win our semis.

Ten–twenty-six. I put a ball in my pocket and serve a fault, take the second out, and serve a double fault. The crowd cheers. "I was sure it would be a fault just looking at the toss," Mariana says. Good serve. Deuce. Long rally from the base line. We punish each other back and forth. In the first set, Connors had more patience. Now it's my turn. Connors hits long. My ad. Then game. 4–1.

Ten-thirty. Connors sneers at baselinesman for an apparently missed call which it was not. Ten–thirty-two. Bad call on my base line, but I win point anyway. Ten–thirty-five. Ball lands an inch past my base line; I don't even swing at ball. Linesman makes no call. 40–30 Connors. Ten–thirty-seven. Jimmy hits forehand I think clips back edge of line. No call. Then Hammond overrules silent baselinesman by calling ball out. Connors protests. Not so much because he wants to get this call changed but in order that he might get a break on the next close one. The same in baseball when a player complains about being called out on a second-base tag; he just wants to get the benefit of the doubt on the next call. Ten–thirty-eight. Connors holds serve, 2–4.

Tennis has had an experimental rule for two years in which umpires can overrule a linesman "if a clear mistake has been made." The problem is that some umpires have interpreted this to mean that they should call every ball themselves—which is not the intent of the rule and has led to chaos in many matches. As Connors said afterward, "Not a match goes by when there is not a squabble. I'm tired of all the bull that goes on. I'm caught in the middle by the uncertainty of officials and my desire to be fair to Bjorn."

After our match, Connors was attacked by linesman Joe Beerman, who said the verbal abuse he received from Connors was "the worst in his twenty years in the game."

There has been a cry for more professional, consistent officiating since open tennis began in 1968. The Eastern Tennis Umpires received $3,800 for the twenty Masters matches; each had a full complement of twelve officials. In addition there was a paid Grand Prix Supervisor at the court for each match. Still, the officiating was a muddle. There is no easy answer. Some nut suggested that if the Eastern Umpires were paid more they'd improve.

Ten-forty. Lennart drys his hand on his wool pants. Match has been running two hours. I win an endless baseline rally to lead 5–2. I'm still not tired. The points are long considering how fast the court is, but not nearly so long as the French Championships, where the slow clay courts make five-setters last five hours. The Supreme Court and the Bancroft balls used at the Garden are faster than I like. The faster the surface, the more it favors big servers like Tanner and McEnroe and good volleyers like Gerulaitis. I would love to have more time to hit my passing shots. Lennart asked an official early in the week—very diplomatically—"Don't you think there would be more rallies on a slower surface?" He's planted the idea. Maybe next year's Masters.

Ten–forty-five. I don't extend myself much on Connors' serve, and he quickly moves to 40–0. This is a standard strategy—one I don't always agree with—to conserve all your strength to serve out the match. One of its problems is that if you get behind on your serve, you may be angry at yourself for letting the other game go so easily. Game Connors, 3–5. Crowd yells support for Jimmy.

Ten–forty-seven. My serve for the match. Connors outsteadies me, 0–15. I'm still thinking how careless I was in the last point when he outlasts me again, 0–30. Damn! Why did I let the last game go so easily. I rifle a forehand uncontested down the line. 15–30. Then a backhand, 30 all. First-serve fault. Long rally when Jimmy changes tactics and charges net. I'm so surprised I rush my passing shot, which goes wide by a full foot. Breakpoint, 30–40. Crowd howls. Hammond calls for quiet.

Connors punishes my serve, which puts me off balance and I make another error after a short rally. Break to Connors, 4–5. Crowd shrieks as we change ends. I've given him too many chances by not hitting hard. I'm just scared.

Ten–fifty-two. Connors grunts loudly and serves a fault. Some jerk high up in the green section screams, "double fault." Connors' second serve just clears the net and I win the rally, 0–15. Another short rally, which Connors wins on my backhand error, 15 all. These are the two shortest exchanges of the night. Maybe we both are beginning to unravel. I make another error this time on a forehand into the net, 30–15. Connors puts a deep first serve to my backhand, and I spin the ball carefully back. Then we begin to work on each other. Side to side. Short angle spinners where the service line meets the sideline and then side to side. The best rally of the match. Finally I hit a good approach, come to net and skid a volley that lands smack on the baseline. Connors races forty feet cross-court and hits a let-cord drive past me. Bedlam, 40–15. I force my return. 5 all. More bedlam.

Damn. He's playing well, but how can I let him come back from 5–2? I've just been pushing the ball back. Can't play safe with Connors.

Ten–fifty-four. Jimmy waiting for me to serve is now skipping an imaginary rope like a prizefighter after the first round. But this is the fifteenth! I hurry my second serve and double fault, 0–15. Then a first-serve fault, and Connors pounces on my shallow second one, 0–30. I have heard of an athlete's wild drive late in a game called an adrenaline flush. It fits Jimmy now.

Ten–fifty-six. Connors spits onto the Supreme Court. I hit a low-percentage drop volley to reach 15–30. Another first-serve fault. But Jimmy overanxious, hits his backhand long, 30 all. First-serve fault. Now I rush my backhand, which lands wide, 30–40. A break point at this stage with Connors' serve to come is considered psychologically a match point. First-serve fault. God, my toss is awful. Low and in front of me instead of high and to the side. Connors just wide with a backhand. Deuce. Connors lifts his head on short forehand and pumps the ball into the middle of the net. My ad. Finally a good first serve. But Connors smacks a forehand return down the line that I can only stare at. Deuce. Connors hurries me with his approach, and I hit into the alley. Ad Connors. It should be my match. I deserve to win. But now he has another break point. I can't believe it.

Crowd boos call as Connors drives just over the base line. Deuce. I can't tell whether the ball was good or out. It was very close. Connors comes in on deep approach and hits a savage volley winner off my pass. Ad Connors. He's impatient again with his forehand—into the net. Deuce. Connors lobs one just long after we have run each other ragged, my ad. Ace, my game, 6–5 final set.

Eleven-two. Another animal shouts "double fault" after Connors hits his first one into the net. I whip a backhand cross-court past Jimmy at net, 0–15. He replies with a backhand down the line that I can't even reach, 15 all. I hurry my backhand, 30–15. Then a Connors' forehand error, 30 all. This was definitely a tension mistake. I hadn't forced him. Long rally, which I lose as my backhand hits the net and trickles into the alley, 40–30. Connors serves first one in and attacks. I attempt a pass down the line, and he hits a lunge volley winner, 6 all. Tie break.

I ace him, 1–0. Connors hits his approach long, 2–0. We rally up and down the sidelines. I beat him twice where the ball is actually past him, but he makes a great recovery and gallops to net only to just miss a volley wide, 3–0. He attacks the net again and swings full bore at a volley, 3–1.

Eleven-eleven. Connors is now relentless. After a short exchange he charges the net and crashes a forehand volley into the corner, 3–2. Connors pays dearly for his next adventure. He comes in on a short ball, which I rip past him, 4–2. Connors bounces the ball four times and faults. Another four bounces and a grunt and the second serve goes in, but the approach shot off my return doesn't, 5–2 to me. Five bounces and a fault, five bounces and a double fault, 6–2. A handful of animals cheer the double. Quadruple match point. Connors like a gored bull keeps charging. He spikes a forehand volley into the clear, 6–3. Now I serve a fault. A dozen fans applaud and another dozen hiss at their rudeness. Crowd noises are

Opposite, my first victory in New York, the 1980 Colgate Masters at Madison Square Garden, was a particularly sweet one.

like a fugue at tournaments. One group will cheer their hero or his foe's mistakes, while the other will respond in counterpoint for their champion's deeds. Another volley winner by Connors, 6–4.

Eleven-fifteen. After a short rally my backhand flicks a let cord. Connors rushes in, but he's too eager and hits his backhand into the alley. What a way to end such a match, but I'll take it now even though I should have closed him out half an hour ago. Game set and match.

Later Mariana speaks to Lennart. "I haven't watched an important match of Bjorn's in four months. I'm not used to it. I've never been so nervous. I think I have to train for my "watching" nerves just as much as Bjorn trains for his "playing nerves.""

After the match, which lasted two and a half hours, I rush to the postmatch press conference, where I remember two particularly dumb questions that were put to me:

"Is this tournament important to you?"

"Was there something missing from your career because you'd never won a tournament in New York before?"

I don't remember my answers.

BJORN BORG'S RECORD ALBUM

1971 & 1972	Winner of the *Orange Bowl Junior Championship* Miami Beach, Florida
1972	Winner of *Junior Wimbledon* over Buster Mottram in finals 6–3, 4–6, 7–5
	Davis Cup—Sweden beats New Zealand. Borg beats Parun 4–6, 3–6, 6–3, 6–4, 6–4; Borg beats Simpson 9–7, 6–4, 5–7, 6–1
1973	Ranks 18 in world
	French Open—Borg beats Riche, Barthes, Stockton; loses to Panatta
	Wimbledon—Borg beats Lall, Hombergen, Meiler, Baranyi; loses to Taylor

1973 (cont.)	*U.S. Open*—Borg beats Barthes, Chanfreau, Ashe; loses to Pilic
1974	Ranks 3 in the world
	$266,160 prize money

Italian Open—Champion
Borg beats Dominguez, Pinto Bravo, Riessen, Orantes, Vilas and Nastase

French Open—Champion
Borg beats Caujolle, Ovici, Rouyer, Van Dillen, Ramirez, Solomon and Orantes (2–6, 6–7, 6–0, 6–1, 6–1)

Wimbledon—Borg loses to El Shafei in 3rd round
U.S. Open—Loses to Vijay Amritraj in 2nd round

1975	Ranks 3 in world
	$226,851 prize money

French Open—Champion
Borg beats Holmes, Szoke, Hrebec, Smith, Solomon, Panatta and Vilas (6–2, 6–3, 6–4)

Wimbledon—Loses in quarter-finals to Arthur Ashe

U.S. Open—Loses to Connors in semi-finals

Davis Cup—Sweden wins Challenge Round first time ever; Sweden beats Poland 4–1

Borg beats Drzymalski 6–0, 6–0, 6–2; Borg beats Fibak 6–4, 6–1, 8–6; Borg/Bengtson beat Fibak/Niedzwieski 6–4, 6–2, 6–4.

Sweden beats Germany 3–2
Borg beats Meiler 6–1, 14–12, 8–6; Borg beats Pohman 3–6, 6–0, 6–0, 6–3

Sweden beats Russia
Borg beats Metreveli 7–5, 6–3, 6–3; Borg beats Volkov 8–6, 6–1, 6–0

Sweden beats Spain
Borg beats Higueras 6–3, 6–1, 6–1; Borg beats Orantes 6–4, 6–2, 6–2

1975 (cont.)   *Sweden beats Chile* 4–1
Borg beats Cornejo 3–6, 6–4, 7–5, 6–3; Borg/
Bengtson beat Cornejo/Fillol 7–5, 6–2, 3–6, 6–3;
Borg beats Fillol 6–1, 6–2, 6–1

Sweden beats Czechoslovakia 3–2
Borg beats Hrebec; Bengtson/Borg beat Kodes/
Zednick 6–4, 6–4, 6–4; Borg beats Kodes 6–4,
6–1, 6–2

1976   Ranks 2 in world
$424,420 Prize money

WCT Dallas Final
Borg beats Dibbs, Solomon and Vilas 1–6, 6–1,
7–5

French Open—Borg loses to Panatta in quarter-
finals 3–6, 3–6, 6–2, 6–7

Wimbledon—Champion
Borg beats D. Lloyd, Riessen, Dibley, Gottfried,
Vilas, Tanner and Nastase (6–4, 6–2, 9–7)

U.S. Open—Borg beaten by Connors in finals
4–6, 6–3, 6–7, 4–6.

1977   Ranks 2 in world
$337,020

Wimbledon—Champion
Borg beats Zugarelli, Edmondson, Pilic, Fibak,
Nastase, Gerulaitis and Connors (3–6, 6–2, 6–1,
5–7)

U.S. Open
Borg defaults to Stockton in fourth round

1978   Ranks 3 in world
$691,886

Wimbledon—Champion
Borg beats Amaya, McNamara, Fillol, Masters,
S. Mayer, Okker and Connors (6–2, 6–2, 6–3)

U.S. Open
Borg beats Hewitt, Gunthardt, Mitton, Solomon,
Ramirez, Gerulaitis—loses to Connors 4–6, 2–6,
2–6.

1978 (cont.)   *French Open*—Champion
Borg beats Deblicker, Fagel, Bertolucci, Tanner,
Ramirez, Barazutti and Vilas (6–1, 6–1, 6–3)

1979   Ranks 1 in world
$1,019,345 prize money

French Open—Champion
Borg beats Pecci 6–3, 6–1, 6–7, 6–4

Wimbledon—Champion
Borg beats Gorman, Amritraj, Pfister, Teacher,
Okker, Connors and Tanner (6–7, 7–1, 3–6, 6–3,
6–4)

1980   As of July 1 ranks 1 in world

Colgate Grand Prix Masters—Champion
Borg defeats Tanner, Connors, Higueras, Mc-
Enroe and Gerulaitis (7–5, 6–2)

TOP SIX PLAYERS' CAREER HEAD-TO-HEAD RECORDS

(THRU MAY 1980)

World Ranking		BORG	McENROE	CONNORS	GERULAITIS	TANNER	VILAS	MATCHES W	L	AV'GE.
1	BORG	–	5	14	17	11	14	61	22	.734
2	CONNORS	10	9	–	15	16	4	54	24	.692
3	McENROE	3	–	3	4	4	3	17	22	.435
4	GERULAITIS	0	3	2	–	4	3	12	42	.222
5	TANNER	4	1	4	1	–	3	13	38	.255
6	VILAS	5	2	4	5	3	–	19	27	.413

BORG'S FAVORITE TEN TOURNAMENTS

DAVIS CUP (all surfaces)
WIMBLEDON (grass)
U.S. OPEN (deco turf-asphalt)
FRENCH (clay)
MONTE CARLO (clay)
TOKYO GRAND PRIX (indoors—fast surface)
BASTAAD (clay)
BARCELONA (clay)
MONTREAL WCT CHALLENGE CUP (indoors—fast supreme)
LAS VEGAS (cement)

I chose these tournaments because they are fun to play and are important to my career. I'd rather play outdoors. I like to do most anything outdoors. It's nicer when it's warm and the sun is shining. Not cold weather. One plays indoors because one has to, not because one wants to.

CHAPTER
10

Finishing Strokes

Tennis has become so popular so fast that its explosive growth is out of control most of the time. There seems to be no direction to the sport—and often every direction at once.

A continual tug of war rages over who has the most influence in tennis. For almost a hundred years, the game was totally controlled by national amateur associations linked together by an austere world body called the International Tennis Federation. They had ultimate power over rules, players, Davis Cup, tournaments—everything. The players had no rights whatever. For example, before 1968, the first year of open tennis, American amateurs were required to return to the U.S. right after Wimbledon for their country's circuit. They had no choice. Furthermore, Americans could compete outside the U.S. only for six weeks a year. Until 1973, European players had to join their nation's Davis Cup or risk suspension.

With the advent of open tennis and the ATP (players' union) the balance of power has swung dramatically to the players. In addition, U.S. antitrust laws have reduced the potency of the U.S. Tennis Association—which once regulated the dates and number of tournaments with a steel fist —to a minor administrative role.

It is true that the out-of-date thinking of the ITF and its

member nations retarded the natural growth of tennis. Do you remember, for instance, the days when the ITF considered a man turning professional the same as turning gangster? But what was substituted for ITF power was not all good either. The ATP did a remarkable job of running the game democratically. Before open tennis, players often got into tournaments by being a friend of the local director or being a good after-dinner speaker. There was no merit system of entry until the ATP developed the first computer world ranking in 1974. Prize money was increased, generous sponsorship was developed and dozens of new tournaments sprang up around the world.

The ATP initiated two programs to regulate and improve officiating. One of a half dozen "supervisors" oversees every single grand-prix tournament to ensure that rules are enforced uniformly around the world. In addition, the ATP runs a school for officials in Dallas and Europe once a year to train linespersons in their controversial skills. Also, the ATP has established a code of conduct with appropriate fines and suspensions for misbehavior. The supervisors, officials' school, and code of conduct are far from perfect, but they are a beginning to correct one of the game's most obvious deficiencies.

I have not always been an enthusiastic supporter of the ATP, because I felt for a long time that it was controlled by Donald Dell, Bob Briner and Jack Kramer, who did not have my best interests at heart. Dell is the lawyer-agent for over fifty pros as well as a promoter of many tournaments, and is the most powerful man in tennis. For years, he was the lawyer for the ATP as well and still controls the ATP's television interests. He does not represent me, and I felt that given a choice he would naturally give an edge to his clients. It may be natural, but I don't think it is fair for someone so close to the ATP to represent players individually as well. Briner was executive director of the ATP for five years and was too close to Dell for my comfort.

Kramer has criticized Jimmy Connors and me in the press for being selfish and not playing enough tournaments, and then he wonders why I won't play his tournaments. Kramer was the first executive director of the ATP but has switched roles from "labor" to "management" and is now the tournament directors' representative from North America to

Opposite, there are lots of things to do outdoors, but let others do the jogging and running.   E. L. SCOTT the Men's Pro Council, which has run the professional game for three years.

The Council is a positive step to clearing the chaos in the tennis jungle. It is formed of nine men—three representatives each from the players, the tournaments, and the ITF, and is headed by Frenchman Philippe Chatrier, who is also president of his own French Association and the ITF. Chatrier is strong and fair, though that is not to say that I agree with him all the time. I don't. Chatrier thinks that Connors, Vilas, McEnroe, Gerulaitis and I play too many "big money" exhibitions that hurt tournaments. He's wrong. Most of our exhibitions are in cities that can't have grand-prix tournaments—or don't want them because they can't be guaranteed top players.

The Council is always trying to devise rules to limit the number of exhibitions we can play. It is wrong to assume that, if I didn't play exhibitions (I play them only four weeks of the year, although I'm permitted six), I'd play more tournaments. I wouldn't. I'd go home to Monte Carlo and rest.

My winning four Wimbledons and four French Opens and Connors' winning the Open three times grant us a privilege that is worth more than the difference between the winner's purse and the runner-up's prize. It is our good luck to be in demand as giant gate attractions for one- or two-night exhibitions. A tournament can't guarantee the public that we'll play each other, and the crowd has to wait a week until the Sunday finals if indeed it does happen. Either of us can lose along the way. Of course, the promoter of an exhibition will pay us a handsome fee simply for our appearance against each other. For anyone to say we should give up this incredible opportunity is crazy.

The opportunity is available only to the top three or four players in the world. We have worked harder and longer than anyone else to get to the top. The suggestion that "for the good of the game" we refuse to play exhibitions is usually put forward by someone who runs a tournament we won't play in.

There are two areas of tennis that are sadly backward. The first is player conduct. The rude gestures and language that have become a standard part of our game is unbelievable. What's the answer? The solution is not, as some believe, to fine the pants off the top players. They make too much money and any fine would merely be treated like a business expense. Suspensions would hurt the game even more because the offenders would be taken away from tournaments already desperate for the top names. If you banned Connors for two months, he'd simply go to South America for an exhibition tour and make more than he could on the Grand Prix circuit.

This is not meant to condemn my friends Connors, McEnroe and Nastase either. They have been seduced into their behavior by total lack of discipline or enforcement procedures in tennis. Further fueling their anger is the fact that there is no answer to the poor standard of line calling, which results in players complaining about good calls that go against them because linesmen have been mistaken so often in the past.

The solution for poor sportsmanship is drastic but simple. Remember when I said that my own temper was cooled forever by being suspended for almost half a year when I was young? We should forget about today's adult tennis pros and work on the younger generation. How? The next time a twelve-year-old tosses his racquet or swears, kick him out of the game for four months. There would be some irate parents for a while, and maybe a few lawsuits, but, if the national associations stuck together, the sorry disease of tennis tantrums would be cured very quickly!

The second major worry is the lack of planning for the future of tennis. The game has never been more prosperous, but no one—not the ATP, the ITF, national associations, sponsors, nor private promoters—has budgeted a penny for a school to train future stars. There should be dozens of international training grounds for juniors, and testing sites for equipment and devices that would improve our sport. One example? Research funds to develop an electronic line-calling device. Also, the machinery for rules changes is creaky and obsolete. For example, in 1975, there were four tie-break formulas used, all officially accepted—Wimbledon's starting at 8 all, the others at 6 all, including the U.S. Open's 12-point and Newport's 9-point "sudden death," and WCT's 13-point.

Our game looked foolish with so many scoring systems. Another thing. How can the ITF ban "spaghetti stringing" and not ban the Prince oversize racquet?

For more than a hundred years, tennis has been alone in not having any restriction on the size or shape of its equipment. A racquet can be ten feet long and made of titanium, but must be conventionally strung. The inconsistency is obvious. Either you permit every racquet, or you specifically detail legal size, shape and material as golf does with golf clubs.

The most-often heard solution for the game's problems is the appointment of a commissioner. The suggestion is naïve. Tennis is so fragmented that no one would give up his feifdom. Open tennis started in 1968 without any structure. In the absence of any organization, a dozen lawyers, agents, officials, promoters and sponsors jumped in to grab a piece of the action—just like a century ago, when American homesteaders rushed in to mark off chosen small parcels of land.

Some of the chaos in tennis has been healthy, in that new ideas have not been slowed down by the type of old-fashioned thinking that stifles the Olympics. The price of our sport's crazy growth has sometimes been total disorder, but one day the dust will settle—without a commissioner. In the meantime, the paying and playing public should ignore our game's occasional predicaments and just go out and hit a few. That's what I'm going to do.

ABOUT THE CO-AUTHOR

EUGENE L. SCOTT, forty-two, is a former member of the United States Davis Cup Team. A graduate of Yale and the University of Virginia Law School, Scott is presently an attorney in New York City. Five times he was ranked among America's top ten players and once reached the semi-finals at Forest Hills. He was the number 1 player in the men's thirty-five rankings for four years.

Gene Scott writes regularly about tennis and has produced four documentary films on the subject for television. He is the publisher and founder of *Tennis Week*, and is a member of the Board of Arbitration of the New York Stock Exchange. He has also lectured for the Practicing Law Institute on various aspects of sports law.